GOD, It's Just Not FAIR!

Or is it?

Toluca Public Library Dist.

By,
J. D. Jenkins

30 Oct 08
May God Bless the
people of Toluca!

J. D. Jenkins †/p

xulon PRESS

Copyright © 2008 by J. D. Jenkins

GOD, It's Just Not FAIR!
Or is it?
by J. D. Jenkins

Printed in the United States of America

ISBN 978-1-60647-510-2

www.xulonpress.com

CHAPTER ONE

S harp, black eyes, sparkling like polished obsidian in the sunlight, scan the ground as the red-tailed hawk cautiously approaches the area where the humans live. Usually he stays away from these contrary creatures, but today, driven by an instinct as old as time itself and abandoning all caution to the wind, he ventures forth, encroaching the airspace over the neighborhoods on the edge of town. While alert for any possible dangers which might present themselves, and yet, eagerly searching for that which he desires, he continues his foray, drifting and circling on the currents of the wind, driven by an instinct as old as the world itself, hunger.

Food is plentiful, back along the tree-lined brook the hawk calls home, but it is also much harder to obtain. It seems like everything which lives far enough away from civilization, not to be partially domesticated by man's close proximity, has senses nearly as sharp as his own. Patience and perseverance have to work in unison to satisfy his internal cravings out there, where even just the slightest shadow can thwart his ravenous desire. Even though the hawk fears the two legged creatures which walk the ground just a short flight from his nest, he is unknowingly patterning his behavior after them. Just like people, he has learned in the past, that there are two ways to do things, the hard way and the easy way.

When it comes to hunting, he is a pro, second to none, but around his own unique residential domain, meals seldom come quickly, for they often dart away, escaping his outstretched talons by mere inches. He must make numerous attempts and face multiple disappointments before success is awarded to his efforts, thus representing, dining the hard way. Just as people prefer doing things the easier way, so too, the hawk has opted today, to eating out in a less physically demanding way. He has learned that in town, he can find a smorgasbord of prey, requiring only the efforts of selection, diving, grasping and devouring whichever creature it is, he chooses to indulge upon. Barring the occasional dangerous interference of the humans, the poor defenseless creatures which catch his keen eyes, usually become his sustenance on the first attempt. Whether it be fortunate for the winged predator, or the misfortune of some young plump animal or tasty bird, those wayward creatures in the town have grown too accustomed to people. Although they still tend to run or fly away from them when they venture too closely, their instinctive reflexes aren't as sharp as their counterparts dwelling out in the wild. Seldom do they stand a chance against the immaculate prowess and aerial proficiency of the proud hawk. Today, he is willing to match his own abilities against the possible perils of civilization in order to gain some scrumptious easy pickin's.

Circling the homes and avoiding the yards with children at play and adults at work, the hawk searches, his hunger growing by the second, until, at last, he has found what he is looking for. Alighting on a dead, broken, maple branch precariously dangling from between the power lines in front of a small house, the hawk balances himself and focuses on the dining selections presented in the yard below. His piercing eyes scan the proximity, and as he tenses his wings, he would lick his lips, if only he had lips, for his dietary selections are plentiful this evening.

Colorful song birds are scattered throughout the yard, but one pair in particular, catches the hawks hungry gaze. Two robins, a brilliantly, bright, red male and a less colorful female, are at play in a birdbath, singing joyfully and splashing around. As the water sprays around them, its many drops, sparkling like diamonds in the sun, they are very much, unaware of the danger overlooking them. A few yards away, in and around an apple tree whose limbs are sagging under the weight of dozens of juicy, red fruits, three fox squirrels are scurrying about. One, with his tail twitching is studiously trying to balance an apple bigger than his head in his mouth as he bounds away from the tree one small jump at a time. He keeps glancing back at the apple tree, appearing as if he hopes that his rambunctious cohorts don't rush over for a bite of his tasty prize, too. He need not worry though, for his frisky companions are much too busy chasing one another and chattering up a storm to be concerned with his apple. Neither he, nor they have any idea of the danger at hand, lurking up in the power lines.

Across the yard in a field of soybeans, something is moving and it catches the hawks attention. Within seconds, another unaware selection for supper materializes which he eyes voraciously. It is a cute gray rabbit with an unusually large white tail visiting the yard, just as she has many times before, to indulge upon the sweet clover growing there. Tonight however, she has not come alone, for much to the hawks satisfaction, one of her brood, a much smaller and tastier version of herself, hops out of the bean field beside her. Decisions, decisions,... what is a hungry hawk to do?

A slight breeze ruffles his tail feathers as the hawk makes his selection, opting for the innocent, unsuspecting squirrel with the apple in his mouth. He has made his way out into the yard just a bit too far from cover and he is so focused on the tasty load he is bearing, that there is no way for him to possibly elude the winged terror preparing to seize him. The hawk poises rigid for a moment, all of his attention zeroing in on the task at hand. He becomes aware of nothing more than the squirrel and satisfying his own voracious appetite. He slowly opens and closes his sharp beak, as if taking a breath and holding it. Suddenly, like a rocket, he swoops off of the dead branch, diving towards the ground and then straightening his approach and gaining speed he aims for the twitching rust colored tail. As fast as the blink of an eye, he is right over the still unsuspecting and defenseless squirrel. He reaches out with his razor-sharp talons, sure of victory when suddenly,... "Wham!" A wooden screen door's slamming, echoes across the yard, announcing the arrival the greatest fear of every bird of prey, a human.

With his hunger instantly forgotten, the hawk veers off course and speeds away to hunt in the safety of his own domain, far away from the dangers of civilization. The two robins who were joyfully splashing around in the bird bath pause for a moment, startled. The squirrels in and near the apple tree halt their activity, not knowing how close they had just come to losing one of their own family. They, and even the rabbits by the field, curiously look towards the door of the house to see who or what is coming.

Without having noticed the hungry hawk, his own belly full from supper, and the dishes done, sixty-six year old Ben Chambers descends the front steps and heads for the group of lawn chairs parked side by side beneath the outstretched limbs of a massive, old, white-oak tree.

If only that tree could talk, oh the wonderful stories it would have to tell, and perhaps its happiest stories, could be derived from the far side of the tree. There, with a newly formed spider web spanning its center, and its creator hanging on for the ride, an old tire swing sways gently in the breeze. Beneath the swing, a furrow of dirt cuts across the lawn, the result of a frequent scuffing of young feet at play. A wooly caterpillar is slowly inching across the bare spot, his coat of colors, forecasting a long cold Winter ahead, for those who believe such things. The shrill chorus of hundreds of crickets beginning to warm up for a night-time serenade, blended along with the sweet melodies of various song birds and the distant hum of a lawnmower, fills the evening air. A refreshing coolness begins to replace the heat of the day.

The field of beans wrapped around the back edge of the yard is almost completely brown now. Soon it will yield its abundant harvest to the hopeful farmer who planted it. The tell-tale signs of Fall are in the air this 3rd of October. The days are steadily getting shorter and the first frost of the year is quickly approaching. A little color shows here and there amidst the green foliage of the trees, but soon the leaves will change and decorate the world with a beautiful array of vibrant colors.

Amazing blends and variations of brown, red, yellow, and orange will adorn the landscape, as if painted by the very hand of God himself. The hummingbirds, songbirds and geese will head South and church chili suppers will emerge, enticing hungry parishioners to indulge their palates upon a vast and delicious selection of homemade delicacies. The distant buzzing of chainsaws will soon be heard resounding throughout the countryside as people prepare their Winter fuel supplies, echoed by the gleeful laughter of children, as they jump in huge piles of freshly raked leaves. Before you know it, costumed boys and girls, dreaming of bags full of candy will be venturing from door to door hollering, "Trick or Treat!" while yet other artistically, creative ornery souls, connive ways to acquire soap and toilet paper for their dastardly evening endeavors.

Soon thereafter, families will be gathering for their Thanksgiving feasts, eating nearly to the point of bursting and having tons of fun. Then the first snow will fall, exciting children of all ages, while at the same time, it will discourage those whom just cannot see the fun in it all. And what then... ? Why,... the most wonderful time of the year, "Christmas" will arrive. Lights, trees, and colorful decorations will almost magically spring up all over the place. Imaginations and expectations will run wild, Christmas music will resound throughout the airwaves, and a great resounding joy will fill all of the earth, or then again, at least it should.

None of this however crosses Ben's mind as he sits beneath the old oak tree. Right now, he is feeling a bit dazed, almost as if he is a prisoner, confined in some sort of trance. He is hardly thinking of anything at all. He stares sadly at the hauntingly empty lawn chair to his left, and his heart pangs deeply within his chest. Ben has experienced his fair share of difficult times, but this is different and he doesn't know what to do. Sarah, Ben's beautiful bride of forty-three years usually can lift his spirits when he is down, but as of late, she too, has been at a loss for how to help him. Plentiful and constant are the prayers she has recently rendered up above for God's healing and comfort. Right now however, she is headed a few miles up the road to pick up the one person who can always get Ben to smile. Even if he doesn't want to feel happy, and no matter how perplexed his thoughts might be, even a down-trodden Ben Chambers couldn't possibly resist the tantalizing charms of the one and only, ever delightful, sweet, endearing and beautiful, Sammi.

At just four years old, sharp as a tack, full of energy and curiosity, and cute and innocent as a new born fawn, Sammi Welsh, has a contagious way of spreading joy everywhere she goes. She's the spitting image of her mother, Amy, Ben, and Sarah's only daughter, with a blend of her father, Joe's, sense for adventure. Tonight, her parents are going to a mega-concert featuring a country music icon who is supposed to be in retirement, and precious little Sammi gets to spend the night at her favorite place, Mammaw and PamPaw's. Ben and Sarah are like putty in Sammi's hands, and despite the fact that she has had them wrapped around her little finger ever since the day she was born, they try not to over-spoil her, and thus, let her know how hooked they are. Like most young children however, Sammi does know how much her grandparents love her and the feeling is quite mutual.

Sammi comes over almost every day and she absolutely loves for Ben to push her in that old tire swing hanging by the lawn chairs. "Again, PamPaw! Again!" she always screeches, while giggling like crazy. Each time, Ben keeps it up until his arms begin to ache, which lately, he has sadly noticed, happens a lot sooner than it used to. Sammi loves to sit in the yard with him counting robins, butterflies, clouds, and most anything her glowing eyes focus on. She looks so much like her mother "Amy" had, at the same age, that Ben is just amazed. She's a precious little bundle of sometimes seemingly endless energy, with dark curly hair cascading down to her shoulders, with a few strands always hanging in her face. Peering from behind them, with long, dark, soft lashes, shines the prettiest green eyes you have ever seen sparkling with the zesty fire of life. She has a slightly up-turned button nose and rosy cheeks, both dotted with light freckles and more often than not, a smudge of dirt or chocolate. Her brilliant white smile, well, it's simply angelic. Her sweet voice is that little-girl voice so full of charm and innocence that it would melt the heart, of even the most cynical, of beings. She constantly asks questions about everything, and in her mind's world, PamPaw is the, "cats meow". She is convinced that he knows everything there is to know, and then some. Sammi has no idea that Ben often doesn't feel smart at all. There are times when he feels like he doesn't know anything at all, and this evening is one of those times. In fact, at this very moment, he is confused and not even thinking about Sammi's momentary arrival.

Ben doesn't notice the two rabbits eating clover near the bean field or the stray dog eyeing the trash can near the road. He doesn't hear the squirrels chattering at one another from the apple tree or even the dragonfly, that has buzzed by him close enough to touch, several times. Even the occasional honking of a passing car driven by a waving friend cannot get Ben's attention. It's highly unusual for him to not be gazing proudly across the immaculate yard, he and Sarah work so hard on, to keep up. Normally, his eyes would be picking out every detail in his surroundings and his mind would be running at about ninety miles an hour. It usually seems as though his mind is in hyperdrive, so full of countless ideas and tidbits of useless information, that Sarah often refers to him as the, "Human Computer." Everyone wants Ben on their team come trivia night down at the church hall because he can always be counted on to have the answers to nearly anything. Ben has lived most of his life on the concepts of, an consistently optimistic view backed by a rock-solid faith in God. He conducts himself with the utmost integrity, always being honest and he has never been afraid of or a stranger to, hard work. Be it so, people naturally come to him for his opinions on things and sometimes, even for spiritual advice. Right now though, as Ben sits somberly in the lawn chair beneath the old oak, hurting, lonely, and confused, he has no advice and certainly, he doesn't have any answers.

Beep!... Beep! The sound of Ben's wristwatch alarm breaks his trance-like state, just long enough for him to notice with surprise, that it's already 7:00 p.m. and the sun is quickly setting. "It's getting late Frrr....?" Ben started to say looking to his left, and the sight of the empty chair stopped him in mid-sentence. Lifting his sad, blue eyes, he looks beyond his yard while a wave of despair encompasses his consciousness once more. He doesn't see the growing, ghost-like shadows stretching across the yard or even the opossum now eating a fallen apple beneath the very same tree, which the chattering squirrels had occupied just minutes ago. Two boys ride by on the side of the road in front of the yard, tossing a football back and forth as they compare their own playing skills to that of their favorite pro quarterbacks, but Ben doesn't hear them. His focus is upon the house and yard adjoining his own property on the left side, that which belongs to Fred and Martha Stone. A faint smile comes to his lips as he notices that although smaller in size, it is kept up as nearly as nice as his own yard, but his smile fades grimly as he speculates, "I wonder if it will stay that way now?" Then suddenly with a surge of anger Ben stiffens up in his chair, sending an unnoticed cricket, that had crept up next to his shoe, scurrying for cover, and he blurts out loud, "God,... It's, It's... It's Just Not FAIR!"

Surprised at his surge of emotion, Ben tries to calm his nerves as he continues to stare at his neighbors small, white, house and he starts to notice things. Black shutters line each of the home's windows and Ben realizes for the first time that one is missing on the window closest to the garage. A piece of siding, up near the eave is discolored and a big yellow tomcat just took off around the house after who knows what. A flower bed full of bright red cannas and chrysanthemums forms a rainbow of colors flowing along the home's foundation and off to one side stands a patch of drooping sunflowers. A deserted birdfeeder, standing like a lone sentry in front of a screened-in-porch on the back of the house, seems eager for the company of the birds who will come to visit it in the morning, if anyone refills it with seed. Looking at the dark screens of the porch, Ben wonders if Martha is hidden behind them, sitting in her rocker and looking out now. What must she be thinking? Is she crying, praying, or is she worried? Ben's heart aches for Martha and he suddenly finds himself praying aloud, "Lord, please help her! Won't you please, help us all?"

Martha and Sarah have been closer than sisters ever since the third grade. For over thirty-three years now, she and her husband Fred, have lived next door, and naturally, Ben and Fred had become the best of friends as well. Over the years, the two couples had become more than just friends and neighbors, they bonded like family. Many were the birthdays, holidays and get-together they had shared together. They belonged to the same community organizations, went to the same church and on many occasions, even went on vacations together. They were always there to share in one another's joys and sorrows, sticking together in both good times, and the bad.

The sun was down to the edge of the bean field now as Ben sat reminiscing over some of the times the two families had experienced together. He mentally pictured a time, just four months ago, when they had driven to the church picnic together. It was a sunny Saturday afternoon and each of them were looking forward to a few hours of food, fun, and fellowship. For Fred and Ben it meant a time of gorging on delicious home-made delicacies, teasing the youngsters, pitching horseshoes and spinning tall tales with the other men. For Martha and Sarah, it would be fun and entertaining, but also a friendly sort of competition with the church's other women. You see, just as in every church, there are certain dishes that each woman is known for and everyone else wants the secret to her recipe. If she brings her signature dish, the other women, even though they would never admit it, are judging it to see if it's up to par. If one of them brings a new dish, then she wants it to be so remarkably delicious, that everyone talks about it, and perhaps even a few, will get jealous. Both Martha and Sarah were part of this friendly ongoing rivalry which has gone on for generations and they take it very seriously. Because of this, Fred and Ben had both known that it was in their own best interest to stay out of the kitchen, or better yet, completely out of sight, until summonsed. Not even on the best of days, did either of them wish to incur the wrath of Sarah or Martha if interrupted while at work in the kitchen on a church picnic dietary creation. That day, things had started out pretty good, or at least for a while.

With the men in the front seat and the women in the back, the drive to the church was one full of idle chatter. After parking, Ben had pulled the trunk release latch and upon getting out of the car, each of them loaded up their arms with the homemade foods and desserts they had brought. Recalling that day, Ben could almost smell the fried chicken and the chocolate-caramel-drizzle cake he balanced in his arms as he closed the trunk lid. As he continued to relive that day from his chair, in the ever darkening shadows of the huge, old oak tree, Ben couldn't help, but smile and laugh aloud as he remembered the hapless look on poor ole' Fred's face, after he had tragically just dropped Martha's prized German potato salad onto the ground. As fate would have it, it didn't land right side up either.

Martha had been six steps ahead of Fred and was just starting to raise her right foot to ascend the church's steps when the mishap occurred. Ben remembered stopping and inadvertently holding his breath as Martha's shoulders stiffened instantly, her right foot slowly sank back to the ground and she turned slowly to stare back at Fred. He helplessly raised his eyes to hers and held his hands, palms upward at his sides smiling weakly. Fred was a slender man with a profound Adam's apple and Ben could remember watching it bob up and down as Fred swallowed nervously waiting for Martha's response. Then after a few tense moments, it happened, making even Ben cringe. Martha gave Fred, "The Look."

Since the dawn of mankind, men throughout the world have come to rue that awful stare, the one with no audible voice, yet it screams, "You Idiot!" Every man within eyesight of what is now known as, "The potato salad incident," hung their heads and looked at the ground feeling the scorn bearing down on poor Fred. He literally looked as though he shrunk in size and wanted nothing more than to crawl into a hole somewhere while under the scrutiny of that awful glare. Each of the other husbands were thanking God that it hadn't been they who dared to have such an accident and each of them took a firmer grip on the culinary masterpieces they were carrying.

Ben had felt so sorry for Fred, but what happened next, made him, everyone else present, and even Martha herself, break out into laughter. Apparently "Jeeters", Pastor Rick's, son's, monster of a golden lab, had been roaming nearby and he was hungry. Still petrified by, "The Look" Fred failed to notice the giant yellow Goliath who was now in front of him devouring the spilled potato salad, as if he hadn't eaten in a month of Sundays. The next thing you know, Fred, still stupified by Martha's brow-beating stare, started to step forward stammering, "Honey, I... I'm... uh...so... Sor... ?" His apology was suddenly cut off as he fell over Jeeters. To make matters worse, Fred was soon covered in potato salad which the famished mongrel was more than obliged to start licking off. Fred resisted the tongue bath at first, but being a big animal lover, and having a great sense of humor, he was soon petting and hugging the big galoot and laughing as hard as everyone else. The church members may have missed out on Martha's famed German potato salad, but they experienced a form of entertainment that money simply couldn't buy. Fred had an amazing way of taking both good and bad times, and making them a whole lot better for everyone.

As Ben turned, once again looking at the empty lawn chair next to his own he sighed and said, "Man, Fred, it's just not right." Then he noticed another spider web, this one stretching from armrest to armrest, and seat to back, of the vacant chair forming a perfectly spun, silky hammock. Resting smack dead in the center was a huge black and yellow garden spider, poised and alert, ready for some aimless insect to become his evening snack. Ben reached down beside his chair to grab a stick with the intent of removing the cunning arachnid, but picturing Fred in this situation for a moment caused him to relent. Looking at the spider, Ben said, "Mr. Creepy Crawly, you just rest easy, because I'm sure that Fred wouldn't mind you a borrowing his chair." In fact, if he were here right now, Ben knew that he probably would have just sat on the ground and watched the spider for awhile.

Fred always said that he loved all, well most of, God's creatures. Ben laughed as he recalled Fred's out-take on insect pests, however. He could just hear Fred's booming, baritone voice now as clearly as though he were seated where the spider was currently poised, "As fer' flies, ticks, skeeters an such, they's a sent to us, straight from Ole Big Red his-self, jest to give us a hard time. Bein' as such, I'd say the good Lord, wouldn't mind if'n we wuz' to make em' fair game fer' the smashin'."

To people who didn't know him, Fred's voice always surprised and even somewhat amused them. It wasn't because of the country jargon he used. Rather, it was because he only stood five feet six inches tall and might have weighed one hundred and thirty-five pounds soaking wet, but his voice sounded like he should have been seven feet tall, weighing in at five hundred pounds and be carrying a club. Ben missed the little galoots giant voice and his friendship.

Standing, Ben stretched a bit and he noticed that it was dark enough now that the yard light was coming on. He heard a car coming down the road and soon a pair of headlights materialized and pulled into the driveway. It was Sarah and within seconds, a blur a of dark, little-girl curls and excitement was rushing across the yard towards Ben, yelling, "PamPaw! PamPaw!" He pushed aside his somber mood from moments ago and donned his biggest smile as he scooped her up into his arms and spun her around three times while saying, "There's my girl! There's my sweet Sammi!"

"Again PamPaw! Again," Sammi exclaimed, and after several more spins, Ben, beginning to feel a bit dizzy, over-dramatized wobbly walking and carried her towards Sarah and the house. He stopped staggering to and fro to give Sarah a big smooch while the bundle of joy in his arms giggled. With great concern showing in her eyes, Sarah asked, "Ben, are you okay?"... Again the sorrow dug at his inner being, but he forced himself to continue smiling and nodded, saying, "I am now, because it's Sammi time!" Sammi's laughing echoed across the yard as Ben tickled his precious cargo and they all three made their way into the house.

The chirping of the crickets continued echoing across the yard as though the family had never been there. A toad came hopping out from behind a rolled garden hose where he had been hiding ever since Sammi first arrived. From somewhere down the street came the faded blast of a car's horn and a lone bicyclist whizzed by, in front of Ben's front yard. The rider never noticed the young skunk which crawled out of the end of the culvert pipe running under the driveway, but that was okay. The skunk was only concerned about the darkness which was quickly enveloping the countryside for it meant one thing, "Supper time."

CHAPTER TWO

"**D**onnnng!... Donnnng!" The mantle piece clock on the fireplace in the living room announced the arrival of 8:00 p.m.. On the television screen sitting across the floor, the latest reality show blared, but aside from furniture, pictures, books, and shelves of knickknacks, the room was empty. The occupants of the house were not yet asleep however, for from the kitchen could be heard a joyous clamor.

If there is one thing that every grandmother knows better than anything else, it is how to make every family members favorite foods. Knowing that Sammi would be spending the night, Sarah had spent part of the afternoon baking, something that she knew was sure to please her beautiful granddaughter, home-made chocolate mint chip cookies. Ben and Sarah didn't have to have their arms twisted behind their backs to admit they liked them as well.

Smeared with chocolate and donning a milk-mustache, Sammi's face, shined like a trophy, thus rewarding Sarah for her efforts, and Ben's similar appearance was like an added bonus. Now wanting to play a game, Sammi was begging, "Go fiss', MamMaw!, PamPaw, go fiss! Pweeeeze!" Ben caught Sarah's eyes and winked at her. "Go Fish" was one of Sammi's favorite games and they played it nearly every time she was over. Wetting a paper towel, Sarah began wiping off Sammi's chocolate mustache and said, "Honey, I have to go check in on somebody, but I'll be back in a little bit to get you ready for bed. You and PamPaw can play, so go get the cards, okay?" The sound of little socked feet drumming down the hallway mixed with an excited answer of, "Okay MamMaw," reverberated through the room as Sammi took off anxiously to find the cards.

Sarah walked up to Ben and with her motherly instincts kicking in, she started dabbing at his chocolate scarred face with the wet paper towel. Standing with his arms at his sides like a big child, Ben rolled his eyes upwards until she was done. Then looking her in the eyes he smiled saying, "Thanks Dear, I guess." Sarah just smiled and replied, "I'll be back in a little bit, I just have to check in on her, you know?" Ben took on a pained expression saying, "Yeah, I know you do. Tell her if there's anything,... anything at all we can do... Well you know?" Walking to the back door and grabbing her jacket off of the hook, Sarah put it on and said, "I will Ben. I won't be long." Ben felt helplessly despaired as Sarah stepped out into the night, but as the door closed, he heard the returning patter of tiny feet behind him. He had to force himself to put on his best fake, "everything's alright" smile, but the expression became genuine when he turned and saw Sammi. She jumping up and down with enthusiasm, as she joyfully brandished the deck of "Go Fish" cards, saying over and over, "Pway' Go Fiss' PamPaw!" And play "Go Fish" they did, having more fun than Ben thought he was capable of having, especially since he had been so sad earlier in the evening. They continued to play, laughing and losing track of the time.

"Do you have a fo', PamPaw," Sammi asked while looking as serious as a poker player at the tables in Vegas. "Go Fish" Ben responded and then he asked, "How about a seven?" Suddenly the back door opened, startling the two card players. For a moment, the evening serenade of insects and a tree frog's solo drifted into the room. The symphony was cut off as Sarah stepped in, closed the door and removed her jacket.

"Hi MamMaw," Sammi hollered with her eyes sparkling. Sarah hung up her jacket and walked over to the table and responded with a smile, "Hello Sammi, Dear! Are you beating

PamPaw at cards again?" The little curly-headed angel just giggled while Ben feigned disbelief and interjected, "Why MamMaw, this little card shark of ours is a kickin' my keister, she surely is! I don't stand a chance of winning." Then with a more serious tone he leaned towards Sarah and asked, "How is she? Is she doing alright? Is she okay?" Sammi's high-pitched voice suddenly cut in, "Who be okay?... Who, PamPaw?"

From the woeful look in Sarah's eyes, Ben surmised the truth as she smiled for Sammi's benefit and replied, "Martha, Honey. She is doing just fine and she said to give you this." and leaning over she gave Sammi a bunch of kisses, which in turn, elicited a tirade of squeals. "Hey, where's mine," Ben asked with a faked urgency as he reached across the table and tickled Sammi. Sarah leaned over to kiss Ben on the cheek and as Sammi continued to giggle, she softly murmured in his ear, "Ben, Martha's taking it so hard that I don't know what we should do? She keeps insisting that she's okay, but her eyes tell me that she's not. She has been crying and looks, just awful. What can we do?" Ben's heart ached as he whispered back, "All we can do is be here for her and pray like there's no tomorrow." He stepped around the table and hugged Sarah for a moment until Sammi piped up, "MamMaw? PamPaw?... Is Fwed still sweeping? I wanna see Fwed!" Sarah's eyes filled with tears instantly and she had to turn away. Ben fought like crazy to control his emotions as pain tore through his heart and he struggled immensely to put on yet another fake smile.

He knelt down looking into Sammi's bright, innocent eyes and said, "Yes Sammi. Fred is still sleeping, but we'll see him again." Ben felt a hard lump suddenly appear in his throat as Sammi asked, "When, PamPaw?... When can we see Fwed?" Ben coughed a little trying to clear his throat as Sarah sniffled and answered for him, "We'll see him later Dear, okay?" That seemed to satisfy the little darling for the time being as she replied, "Okay MamMaw," and then in her sweetest voice she said, "I wike' Fwed! I wike' Fwed Fwinsone." Ben forced a gentle laugh as he grasped Sarah's hand and tousled Sammi's hair. You see, although not many people knew it, the "F" in Frederick F. Stone actually did stand for Flint and Sammi loved kidding him about that. Ben pictured his best friend laughing under the big old oak out in the yard as he and Sammi teased one another, like they had so many times over the Summer. Looking at Sarah, Ben added, "Me too Sammi! I really like Fred Flint Stone too."

According to the clock on the stove, it was going on 8:15 p.m. and the microwave read 8:17 p.m.. Sarah didn't notice either of these, but the clock on the dining room wall, which she did glance at, matched the one hanging on the wall above the kitchen sink. They both said that it was 8:18 p.m. and well past a certain little girls bedtime. She said, "Well, young Ms. Welsh, it's time for someone to get cleaned up and go nighty-night." Ben couldn't help but to laugh a little as he watched Sammi. She was winding down quickly, rubbing her eyes, stretching her little arms and trying to stifle a yawn. She said, "But Mamaw, I not tar'd" and she kept on saying that she wasn't tired as she yawned again and again as she followed Sarah down the hall.

Ben went into the living room and settled down into his well worn recliner. A singing reality show was on the tube and he quickly turned the channel. Ben and Sarah had both enjoyed the show in it's first few years, but by now it was more like, "Ho hum. Seen that. Next channel." He spent a few minutes watching an old western, but he just couldn't get into it. Ten minutes of a mud-slinging political campaign speech made him feel more depressed and even the medical drama, he and Sarah usually watched and enjoyed each week at this time, wasn't able to gain his attention. Out of one hundred and fifty premium satellite channels, Ben could find nothing interesting enough to lift his thoughts from out of the cauldron of sorrows, in which they had been submersed, these past three days. That's how long it had been, nearly eighty-six hours since the, horrifying, unthinkable accident. As he began to picture that day Ben shook his head and fought to keep back the wall of tears forming behind his eyes. "I just don't understand, Lord. Why Fred," he uttered softly as he sunk into deep contemplation.

Ben, abruptly awakened to reality as a little green-eyed princess in pink pajamas with butterflies all over them suddenly plopped into his lap, smelling like soap and strawberry shampoo. She had her brown, one-eyed teddy, which she had curiously named, "Hiccup", in tow. Why Sammi had chosen that name for her soft and cuddly friend was anybody's guess. Ben could tell that Sammi was tired, but before she went to bed, she wanted PamPaw to tell her a story. She threw her arms around his neck as he rocked forward to get up out of the recliner. Success was awarded to him on the third attempt. From across the room, Sarah had appeared and was laughing, amused at his efforts. She walked over and put her hand on the small of Ben's back, following him down the hall as he carried his precious cargo down to her very own special private bedroom.

The room had been Amy's when she was growing up, decorated in the fashionable fads of the late eighties and early nineties. When Amy went off to college, and even after she married Joe, the room changed very little, but shortly after Sammi was born, Ben and Fred, under the somewhat tedious direction of Sarah and Martha had remodeled the room. Down came the movie posters, pictures of past alleged teen heart-throbs and the dusty shelves bearing a curious assortment of books, trophies, knick-knacks, little raisin characters which had once been given out in a fast-food restaurants promotional campaign and all kinds of plastic jewelry. There was an old six sided game cube with half of it's colored stickers missing, an old plastic clothes hamper full of stuffed animals and all kinds of half used or dried up bottles and containers which had once held various make-ups and perfumes. In one of the dresser drawers, behind a pile of mismatched socks there was a big plastic cup from a theme park with a picture of 1991's new roller coaster wrapped around the outside. It was full of dust-covered coins, paper clips, earrings, and even a few old pieces of individually wrapped candy. Out of curiosity, Fred had decided against Ben's better judgment, that he should try a piece of it. After he spent nearly four minutes prying off the faded paper wrapper, Ben nearly split a gut laughing, when his sweet-tooth-challenged friend spit out the ancient candy and rushed to the kitchen for a drink of water.

Between the mattress and the box-springs of the bed, nearly thirty long-forgotten, love-notes from one of Amy's high school admirers had been stashed away along with a "D-" Algebra paper, which oddly, Ben and Sarah had never knew of. Under the bed, amidst a colony of cobwebs and dust bunnies, they found an old cereal box full of pictures and all kinds of shoes from size six to eight and one half. Beneath the shoe assortment, they uncovered and old stamp collection and some teen magazines.

The closet held an assortment of old clothes, more shoes, puzzles with missing pieces, board games, and a large pink frilly top hat with "papier mache" roses all over it which Amy had wore to school on, "Crazy Hat Day." Ben had dared Fred to try it on, and of course, since one has to accept a dare, when presented, Fred put it on and started prancing about the room. Ben was about to introduce to a make-believe audience, the red carpet arrival of one, "Madamemoiselle Frederica," when Sarah and Martha suddenly walked into the bedroom. The two women stood stunned for a second or two just staring at Fred unable to believe what they had just happened in upon. Then, the combination of a bewildered shake of her head and quite a different version of, "The Look," from Martha followed by Fred immediately throwing the hat off as if it were on fire, while turning three shades of red with embarrassment, caused Ben to break out laughing hysterically. Sarah, unable to contain herself, broke out laughing as well stating, "Where's a camera when you need one?" Then she looked at Ben with a "I know you put him up to it." stare. It was quite a while after that before he could get Fred to take him up on any more dares.

Having literally no idea of what Amy would want to keep and what she would choose to throw away, Ben and Fred just boxed up everything, even a dust-bunny covered sock, just for laughs. It took an entire day for the two men to clear out Amy's old room and Joe had to bring over his pickup truck to haul all of her stuff home. Later, when he and Amy started going through her childhood mementos, they had a blast poking fun at and reliving things long past, but there was so much of it, that even today, several unopened boxes are at the back of their guest bedroom's closet.

By the end of a second day, Ben and Fred were feeling pretty good about their progress on the bedroom remodel. The furniture was all out in the garage, and the worn, dark pink carpet that had covered the floor was rolled up along with the old padding, by the garbage cans near the road out front of the house for the sanitation guys to pick up. That morning, the bedroom's walls had been lavender in color with pieces of tape, thumb tacks, staples, and pinholes all over them. By that evening, they were smooth and clean, with a fresh, double coat of white primer, as was the closet door. It had previously sported a red-markered heart on the back with an inscription which had read, "Amy -X- Billy, Doug, Chris, Stanley." Ben had no idea the heart existed before, or of who any of the boys had been, but it was apparent that Amy had changed her mind a few times. She didn't meet Joe until she was away at college.

Ben and Fred both found out over the next few weeks however, that Amy's prerogative to change her mind paled in comparison to that of her mother's and Martha's. Even though the wives tended to think alike, they seldom agreed with their husbands when it came to decorating a little girl's room. They had to take the women to five different home improvement stores, three paint centers, four carpet outlets and two interior furnishing stores before they were able to get all of the materials they needed to finish little Sammi's room. They actually even had to paint the walls of the room, three different times, and bite their tongues at least two hundred times in order to get the job done satisfactorily and somehow still maintain marital bliss. Ben hired a local carpenter to do the finish work and a friend to lay the carpet whom was in the business. It was kind of funny, but when it came to hanging pictures and placing the furniture in the room, Sarah and Martha would ask for each other's opinions, but rather than ask Ben and Fred theirs, they tended to tell the men how it was going to be and then inadvertently blame them if they didn't like the results. It wasn't easy or fun for the men, but now, every time Sammi comes over and sleeps in her room, Ben knows that it was all worth the effort. He's definitely in no hurry to do any more remodeling anytime soon though.

Now the carpet is a crème colored berber and the walls are a hot pink with white wainscoting and woodwork. The bed is a small poster type with a butterfly comforter, big, soft pillows, and at least a dozen stuffed animals on it. There is one window in the room facing towards the big oak tree in the yard and its curtains match the bed. On the wall over the bed is a picture of Jesus tending a flock of sheep. There are three other pictures in the room, one of Sammi as a baby, one of she and her parents at a baseball game from a season ago, and another picture which was only one month old. It was of Sammi, Ben, Sarah, Martha, and Fred each holding cotton candy while standing in front of a huge Ferris wheel at the county fair.

Butterfly border runs around the room's walls, just under the ceiling and three light pink rugs are spread about the room. Along one wall is a white dresser and a toy crib with some of Sammi's baby dolls in it. Against another wall is a small white bookshelf with her favorite books, some cartoon figurines, a children's Bible, and a little butterfly purse on it. A full length mirror is mounted to the closet door and even the light switch and outlet covers and night-light have butterfly designs on them. It's a good thing that Sammi loves butterflies! On the back of the door leading into the hall, hangs a cross that Fred and Martha gave Sammi when she was baptized.

Tonight, Sammi's eyes never leave Ben's as he lays her on the bed, not even when Sarah pulls the covers up under her chin. Her sweet voice is tired, but insistent as she says, "Stowy PamPaw! Wead' me a stowy!" Looking at her with his heart full of love, Ben bargains, "Say your prayers first Honey, and then I'll tell you a story, okay?" Sammi tries unsuccessfully to stifle a yawn as she replies, "O..., okay PamPaw." Ben and Sarah hold onto one another enjoying the comfort of one another's loving embrace as she utters her prayers in a tired voice they can barely hear.

"Dear Jesus. Tank you fo' MamMaw an' Pampaw. Tank you fo' mommy, Daddy and fo Hiccup. Tank you fo' "Go Fiss", an cookies an fo' Fwed. Pweese help him sweep okay, an me too! Amen." Ben squeezed Sarah a little tighter as Sammi prayed that last part and then smiling down at her he asked, "Okay Sammi, what kind of story would you like me to tell you?" Sammi looked up through half closed eyes and said, "Tell me bout' Fwed. Was Fwed always yer bes' fwend, PamPaw?" The pain hit Ben again as he took a seat on the edge of Sammi's bed. Sarah placed her hands on his shoulder as he tried to maintain his composure, and looking at his precious granddaughter he began his story. He had to cough a little to get started, but he was bound and determined not to let Sammi see his sadness. He answered, "Actually Sammi, Fred wasn't always my best friend, but Martha and your MamMaw here, have been best friends since the third grade. Let me tell you however, about the first time I saw Fred, it's pretty interesting." Ben's mind began to wander back as he continued, "It was on Christmas Eve, back in 1972, when Amy,… I mean when your mom was the same age as you are now."

"Mommy was fo," Sammi asked half asleep. Ben smiled at Sarah as he went on, "Yes, she was four and we were in church watching the children's Christmas Eve program." Sammi yawned again with her eyes closed and she mumbled, "I wike' Cwismas." Mentally picturing that church service, Ben continued in a softer voice, "The children had just finished their part in the program and our old pastor back then, Pastor Miller, was getting ready to say a prayer, but we noticed that he seemed preoccupied. He kept glancing over our heads and towards the double doors at the back of the sanctuary. I remember him saying, "May we bow our heads." and as we did, he suddenly said, "Just a minute folks." We were all confused as we watched him step down from the altar area, walk down the aisle and disappear through the double doors." Sammi mumbled something that sounded like, "H… he…dis… disa… perd?" Ben and

Sarah exchanged glances, smiling at each other as Ben stood up and whispered, "Yes, Sammi Dear, he disappeared." Bending over, they each placed a kiss on Sammi's forehead and they quietly exited the bedroom as their wonderful granddaughter drifted off into the mystical realms of dreamland.

Ben spent the next half hour or so shaving, cleaning up, and getting ready for bed while Sarah took a turn at trying to find something worthy of viewing on the tube. The clock on the mantle was chiming nine bells as Ben came into the living room. Sarah was watching the end of a weight-loss reality show and after a few minutes of idle chatter, she went down the hall to go through her own set of nightly rituals before going to bed. Ben felt exhausted, the way a person does after a day filled with stress and sorrow, as he plopped down into his recliner. Grabbing the remote off of the coffee table next to his chair, he started flipping through the channels once more until he found a program showcasing the building of a huge Dam somewhere on the other side of the world. He was just getting good and comfortable when a commercial for hot-chocolate appeared on the screen. "Why did they have to go and show that?" Ben surmised aloud, as he lunged twice to get out of his chair and head to the kitchen. He had a passion for hot chocolate, especially the kind with the little marshmallows in it.

A few minutes later, Ben sat a steaming mug of cocoa on the coffee table and fell back into his chair. As fate would have it, his leg hit the table, not hard, but with just enough force, to splash hot chocolate out of the cup and onto a picture standing beside it. Ben grumbled as he heaved his way out of the chair once more to go get a paper towel, and as he wiped the picture off, for some reason, a vision of Fred entered his mind. It was the time Fred spilled a steaming hot cup of coffee in his lap at the "Bingo Hall" down town and everyone there mistook his jumping up and yelping in pain, as a winning "Bingo" call. Ben chuckled at the vision, but almost instantly, sorrow was knocking at the door of his heart once more. He started thinking about the bedtime story he had been telling Sammi earlier. He laid the chocolate-soaked paper towel on the coffee table and carefully sat back down in the recliner. He took a long slow sip of the cocoa, savoring it's flavor and settled back no longer interested in the building project on the television screen. Ben sighed, but he wasn't aware of it, for in his mind, he had traveled back in time, to that Christmas Eve long ago. He was once again sitting in a pew with his family at the church, looking back at the double doors which Pastor Miller had just disappeared through. Once again he was reliving that very special and remarkable Christmas Eve in 1972.

CHAPTER THREE

Hushed whispers could be heard coming from around the sanctuary as the curious congregation stared at the back of the room. "Where did he go?"..."What's going on?"... "What's happening?" As the murmurings rose, one man suggested with a little chuckle, "Maybe he had to use the rest room?" The comedian received one of those, you know, "Looks" from his wife followed up by a sharp elbow and the proverbial, "Shhhh!" One child whispered excitedly, "Maybe he saw Santa Claus?" Well, it wasn't jolly old St. Nick whom had gotten the preachers attention, but moments later when Pastor Miller came back into the room, he wasn't alone. He was leading a man up the aisle whose very appearance cast the room into a stunned silence as nearly every mouth dropped open in surprise.

Pastor Miller might as well not even been in the room for every pair of eyes was focused on the individual behind him. He was a skinny chap of medium height, but it was impossible to determine his age. He had a slight limp and walked hunched over, with his head down and his hands clasped tightly in front of him. Unraveled strings hung down from his stained, tattered stocking cap, and it was anybody's guess as to what color it once had been. His dark hair was a wild, tangled, and dirty mess, dangling well past his shoulders and hiding most of his scraggly beard covered face. His hands and what you could see of his face, were covered with cuts, scrapes, and bruises, but you could see none of these, for he was nearly black with dirt and grime. He wore an old Army jacket, with "Staff Sergeant" rockers on the sleeves, dirty ripped jeans, and from his discolored, clenched fingers hung a filthy, tattered knapsack. A closer look would have revealed that the man had no socks and he was wearing an old, dingy tennis shoe on one foot and a different sized work boot with a broken lace on the other.

Hushed whispers started drifting through the chapel as the pastor led the stranger all of the way to the front row where Ben, his family, and Sarah's best friend, Martha Whitmoore, were sitting. After a glance and quick jerk of the head by Pastor Miller, they all scooted down the pew to make room for the unkempt visitor. The pungent odor of grime and a long unwashed body clung to the man like a shadow as he sat down, with his head hung low. Ben felt sorry for him and wondered what had happened to him. He felt the urge to say something, even just to utter a welcome to him, but the man's offensive odor and appearance, prevented him from doing so. Pastor Miller, bless his soul however, had gotten back up in front of the congregation and he started praying as if nothing had happened. Only a few heads were bowed in prayer throughout the church though, for an overwhelming sense of wonderment now filled the curious minds of the staring parishioners.

Seemingly oblivious to the attention focused in his direction, the poor stranger just continued to stare downward with his hands still folded tightly together. "Surely he can hear them?" Ben thought as whispers made their way to his ears. He heard things like, "Who is that dirty man?"... "Phew! He needs a bath."... "George! Stop staring at him,"... and a whole lot of shushes. Ben had to fight the temptation to stare at the man and he tried to tune his hearing in to the pastor's prayer. Then Ben heard Amy whisper to Sarah, "Da' poor, poor man, Mommy. He needs Baby Jesus for Cwismas." Sarah looked at her daughter and whispered back, "Shhhh! Yes Honey, we all need Baby Jesus." Ben glanced at the stranger out of the corner of his eyes to see if he had heard. The poor man seemed to be mumbling something incoherent, and he was slowly rocking forward and back. Ben realized that he was praying. "What is he praying?" Ben silently wondered.

Suddenly the pastor raised his voice and Ben remembered that he was supposed to be praying also. He closed his eyes and tried to focus on what Pastor Miller was saying. He kept going on and on and Ben suddenly realized that he was doing it intentionally. He was throwing everything into that prayer he could think of to get the congregations focus off of their newest visitor and back onto celebrating the birth of the Christ child. Finally, he reached the end and on the echoes of 'Amen' sounding throughout the room all of the church's lights were turned off except for a big lighted star atop the Christmas tree.

For as long as anyone could remember a huge pine or cedar, stretching from the floor to mere inches from the cathedral ceiling was erected and decorated in the front right-hand corner of the sanctuary. Hanging in its branches were hundreds of ornamental symbols which all held meaning in the church's season of Advent and strings of white lights. Since he was a boy, Ben had participated nearly every year in locating the tree, cutting it down, and transporting it to the church and decorating it.

He even enjoyed being the yearly volunteer for attaching the lighted star on top, but some of the other men often secretly questioned his sanity in this. You see, in order to get the star on top of the tree, it had to be done off of an extension ladder. Of course you couldn't lean the ladder against the tree so you had to decorate with faith. You had to have faith in God that you wouldn't fall, faith that the two or three men holding the base of the ladder wouldn't lose their grip and faith in the group of men holding the ropes tied to the top of the ladder would not let it fall. Each year as Ben scaled the ladder, the men holding the ropes would let the ladder lean towards the tree until he could reach the top. You never knew though, when the rope guys might decide to pull a practical joke, which they frequently threatened to in a friendly way, but Ben knew that he was safe in their hands and he always thoroughly enjoyed placing the star.

The sanctuary was silent and peaceful as everyone stood and looked up at the tree's shining star. For many churchgoers, this was their favorite part of the Christmas Eve service. It was Ben's as well. It was often at this very time, that the true meaning and joy of Christmas came to light in the hearts of many of the people. They felt like all of the rushing and preparation was done and they could finally let the joy of the season come charging in. At that very moment however, Ben had no idea just how clearly the true meaning of Christ's birth was going to ring true in he and his family's life, but he was soon going to find out.

The church's old pipe organ started to belt out the music for "Silent Night" and soon, everyone was singing. The first few verses were in English, but true to an ancient tradition in the church, one or two verses were always sung in "German." Ben himself had never quite mastered the German language, so he took advantage of that opportunity to gaze at the mysterious stranger sitting beside him. Ben was totally captivated by what he saw as the congregation started singing, "Stille Nacht, heilige Nacht, Alles schlaft....!"

Something stirred deep inside of Ben's soul. He could feel a great wave of anguish, pain and despair mixed with, what felt like an intense desperation coming from the man next to him. In the faint glow cast by the star on the tree, Ben saw that he was staring upward with anguish and desperation, his arms raised in complete surrender. His hair was pulled back from his face and great tears were cascading down from his grief-stricken eyes. His body was convulsing with passion and Ben, unable to turn away, no longer saw the torn clothing, the dirt or the long unkempt hair. He became unaware of the foul odor surrounding the poor, distraught soul, and he no longer viewed him as a stranger. He didn't even wonder what great burden must be tormenting the poor man's inner being. All Ben could do was stare at the man, whose eyes looked up to something beyond the lighted star, silently, but desperately seeking, searching and begging for God to save him and to love him.

Ben surmised for just a second or two, that the longing he could see in the man's tear filled eyes, must have been like that in the eyes of the Magi many years ago, when they too looked towards a bright shining star in the Eastern sky. Long before, prophecies had told of it and they eagerly ventured towards the star, hoping and believing, that in its light, they would find the answer to all of their prayers.

As the congregation continued to sing, "Stille Nacht, Heilige Nacht, Gottes Sohn, o wie lacht…!", something totally amazing and miraculous took place. Suddenly, Ben realized with a start, that he could understand the German singing. They were singing, "Lieb' aus deinem got lichen Mund, Da uns schlagt die rettende Stund'. Christ, in deiner Geburt! Christ, in deiner Geburt," but what he heard was, "Radiant beams from thy holy face, with the dawn of redeeming grace, Jesus, Lord at thy birth, Jesus, Lord at thy birth!" Ben knew upon later reflection that he had witnessed a miracle. The miracle however, wasn't his sudden comprehension of a foreign language. It was the realization and visualization of the true meaning of Jesus birth and the power of his love. Ben witnessed its life-changing ability at work first-hand, in the both the physical and spiritual metamorphosis of forlorn stranger visiting the church that wintry evening. It was a night that he most definitely, would never forget.

He watched mesmerized, as a magnificent transformation came over the troubled brother in Christ standing next to him. Ben had been a Christian and loved Jesus all of his life, but never before, had he felt as he did that Christmas Eve. Like magic, the sadness, remorse and anguish he saw in the man's eyes slowly disappeared and was replaced at first, with an odd sense of curiosity. It appeared as though someone were speaking to the man in a voice which only he, could hear. He appeared to be listening so intently that Ben found himself looking up towards the star where the man seemed to be looking, and he strained his ears to hear whatever it was that the man was hearing. Ben was so transfixed by what was happening just a foot to his left, that he no longer was even aware of the church's music, the people singing or much of anything, rather than the phenomenon occurring beside him.

He nearly jumped out of his skin when suddenly, the man's eyes opened wide and flashed a look of awesome surprise. "What is he hearing, Lord?... What in the world is going on?" Ben's thoughts screamed, as he desperately looked to the star and back at the changing appearance of the man. Then, after what happened next, Ben somehow inwardly knew what was going on and it made him feel great! The change taking place in the stranger wasn't of this world, it was of a Heavenly magnitude.

The man's countenance changed right in front of Ben and appeared to glow and then, something, yet even more amazing, changed in his eyes. The curiosity and surprise that had replaced the sadness and anguish, which had been there a moment ago, was then replaced with what Ben could only later describe to Sarah as, a holy blend of tender compassion, true understanding, soft and humble acceptance, insurmountable jubilation, thankfulness, and a pure form of peace and love only capable of coming straight from God, himself. Tears, not of sorrow, but of a great joy started cascading down the man's face and Ben became aware that he was shedding a few of his own as well. Right there next to him in the church pew, Ben witnessed the acceptance of our Savior's forgiveness and love in such a way, that he suddenly seemed to truly realize the true meaning of Christmas for the first time in a way that he never even had considered before. It was perhaps, the most amazing thing he had ever experienced and it changed his life forever. Ben felt his own heart swelling with of all things, gratitude. He reached out, placing his hand on the redeemed man's shoulder and smiled. The man turned, looking at Ben through tear-filled eyes. His lips were trembling and without saying a word, but his radiant face told Ben what he already knew, that Jesus had just saved another lost soul.

Ben felt a tug at his hand and he looked down to see Amy, who was urgently pleading, "Wet's go Daddy!" He became aware that the congregation had stopped singing and people were beginning to exit the pews. Salutations of, "Merry Christmas!" began to resound throughout the room and soon the church's trustees were busy by the back doors, handing out bags of goodies to children of all ages. Smiles abounded in every direction while the excited banter of children filled the air in harmonious accord with the organ which was still softly silently playing, "Silent Night." Sarah glanced over the top of Amy's head, smiling at Ben and wishing him a Merry Christmas. He returned the greeting with a smile, somehow knowing that she hadn't seen what he had just witnessed. Later, he would share it with her, but as for now, he just silently uttered a, "Thank you Lord" towards Heaven. Again an overly-anxious Amy was tugging at his hand exclaiming, "Cwismas Daddy, at MamMaw and Pampaw's. It Cwismas Daddy! Come on Daddy, wet's go!... Wet's go!" Ben was still a bit dazed by the miracle he had just seen, but he quickly snapped back into the here and now and started teasing and tickling Amy until she started giggling hysterically.

Ben looked around the room to see if he could tell if anyone else had seen the poor visitor's miracle, but for some reason, he was not surprised that it appeared no one else had. The stranger was standing in the aisle now, still looking up towards the star on the tree as Ben exited the pew. The man turned towards him with a smile as Ben extended his hand saying, "Merry Christmas Brother! I'm Ben Chambers and that beautiful woman back behind me is my wife, Sarah. This pretty little bundle of giggles and energy beside me is my four year old daug...," suddenly, Amy pushed her way past her father and made her own introduction as she held out her little hand and exclaimed, "Mawwy Cwismas mista'! I'm Amy." The man looked at Ben and Sarah with a wink and then he stooped down in front of Amy gently grasping her extended hand and he smiled from ear to ear. Ben and Sarah looked at each other in surprise when he spoke, for although he appeared to be a man of small stature, his voice was deep, like that of a great giant. He said, "My, my, young Ms. Amy Chambers! I'm quite pleased to make your acquaintance and might I offer you, a most splendid and wonderful salutation of, Merry Christmas! My name is Frederick F. Stone, but you can just call me Fred."

Amy clasped her little hands and blushed for a moment smiling. Then with a giggle and her sweet young voice teeming with excitement she said, "Okay Fwed!" Turning to Ben, she said, "Daddy, Mista' Fwed knows Jesus!" As Fred straightened back up, he and Ben exchanged knowing glances. Then adopting a little more countrified vernacular, he said, "Reckon yer pert near right bout' that Lil' Darlin', ah' sho nuff does know Jesus." Ben shook the man's hand again, somewhat surprised at the strength in his grip. Somehow, Ben knew inside that he had just met his future best friend.

Sarah reached around Ben to offer Fred her hand. She smiled as she shook his hand wishing him a Merry Christmas and then she introduced him to Martha, saying, "Mr. Stone, this is my good friend Martha Whitmoore." Martha, whom like Sarah, was thirty-one years old at the time, was the sweetest woman you would ever want to know. She was a quiet, petite brunette with average looks, a cheerful smile, and dimples. She was un-married and both of her parents had passed away. She had no close relatives, but she considered Ben, Sarah, and Amy Chambers, as her adoptive family. Martha lived in her parents old house which just so happened to be right next to theirs.

Several times in the past, Sarah had tried to play matchmaker for Martha, but nothing had ever worked out. Although she tried not to let it show, Martha secretly feared that she was destined to be an old-maid. She had plenty of opportunities to meet possible suitors while working as a waitress at "Ma's Diner" in town, but unfortunately, "Mr. Right" had not yet come in for a meal at any of her tables.

Most of her evenings were spent alone crocheting, reading her Bible or watching the tube. When she did go out, it was usually to church functions or on family outings with Ben, Sarah and Amy. Going with them to drive-in movies was one of her absolute favorite past times. She always found herself mesmerized by the action and drama presented on the huge movie screen. For a few hours she could forget being single and lonely and lose herself in the imagination of being someone else, in another place and doing things she had never even dreamed of before. She also would have had to admit that she enjoyed sharing popcorn and other treats with Amy and pushing her on the swings under the outdoor screen. Listening to her squeals of merriment, tended to make Martha feel like a child again herself. Ben and Sarah had almost as much fun watching the two of them play, as they did doing it.

Martha spent every birthday, holiday, and many evenings and weekends with their family, cherishing every second that she didn't have to be at home alone. She often tried to convince herself that God himself, was keeping her company and that when the time was right, he would waltz the answer to her lonely prayers right into her life. But, some days she just wasn't so sure that her own knight in shining armor, "Prince Everything" would ever come along. Even Sarah had no idea of how many times Martha had cried herself to sleep. Martha had become an expert at putting up a good front, convincing everyone that she was doing better than she actually was. It became very apparent however, on that Christmas Eve in 1972, at the church, underneath the big tree with the lighted star, that God truly did see through her feeble façade. He even knew the secret desires of her heart, even better than she herself, did.

Outside, it was cold and just enough snow covered the ground to make everything appear like a perfect post-card Christmas. Inside the church however, hearts were warmed by the celebration of Christ's birth, and Ben's more so, by the witnessing of Fred's awe-inspiring miracle, but the surprises were not yet over. Following Sarah's introduction, came a moment when time, if even only for a moment or two, seemed to stand still for both Martha and Fred. The old adage was proven once more, "God does truly work in mysterious ways" for when their eyes met, it definitely became a Christmas Eve to remember.

Although Ben, Sarah and little Amy were still standing right there, they might as well been somewhere out in outer space, because Fred and Martha were frozen momentarily. Their eyes were locked and they had became aware, only of one another's presence. Simultaneously, their mouths dropped open and waves of glorious emotion washed through their inner most being. Their hearts pounded reverently in unison and each of them inwardly felt as though they were gazing upon the one missing link which had been absent in each of their lives for so long. Great joy for what may be, mixed with an even larger wave of panic and fear for daring to believe that it might be possible, hit them both.

"She's so beautiful!… Hey!… Come on Fred, ole' boy, snap out of it!… Say something," Fred's mind screamed at him after a few seconds of stunned silence. Suddenly it seemed to be growing hotter in the church and it became difficult to breath. Mustering all of his self control, and desperately trying not to reveal the roller coaster ride of emotions that his heart was riding on, Fred finally stepped around Ben, Sarah and Amy to face Martha. Without taking his eyes off of her, he slowly extended his hand and in a deep, cultured and gentle voice he said, "Good evening Ms. Whitmoore and may I wish you a Merry Christmas." As their hands joined, an electricity flowed through them that was so obvious that it even caused Ben and Sarah to exchange a surprised, but knowing glance. Then Fred did something which perhaps, should have seemed odd, but somehow it did not. While still holding Martha's hand, which she was made no attempt to withdraw, he bent at the waist, still keeping his eyes locked onto hers and he said, "I am most honored to meet you" and he kissed the back of her hand. Now it was Ben and Sarah's turn to be frozen in time as they awaited with abated breath, wondering how Martha was going to respond.

You would think ordinarily, that someone placed in this situation would have drawn back quickly, startled or maybe even repulsed by Fred's crude appearance. After all, remember that he was a total mess. He was not in the least, a magnate of physical attraction. He was dressed in filthy rags, with mismatched shoes, long unkempt hair a long neglected beard and his skin and nails were so dirty that you could no longer tell their true color. He smelled so awful that it would make you cringe your nose from twenty feet away, and to top it all off, he was a complete and total stranger, right? Who knew? He might have been a vagabond, a fugitive from the law or the very guy whom every mother has warned her daughter about. He could very well have been trouble with a capitol "T", but none of these thoughts entered the minds of any of that small group still standing in the front row of pews in that little church.

The fact is, that when God wills it to be so, love really can occur at first sight, and that that night it did. Martha was still so caught up in the moment that she was unable to speak, but the sparkling in her eyes and the amazing smile that spread across her face told more than words ever could. Suddenly, the romantic spell was broken when Amy started tugging on Ben's hand anxiously exclaiming, "Cwismas at MamMaw an' PamPaw's, Daddy!... Wet's go!... Wet's go!" Everyone laughed and started to head into the aisle when Amy quickly darted up to Fred, grabbed his filthy hand and said, "Come on Fwed!... Wet's go ta' PamPaw n' MamMaws fo' Cwismas!"

Once again, at that juncture in the evening, is when most people might have thrown up the caution flag, for they still didn't really know Fred, but God was apparently was not yet done with his children that evening. Following Amy's unprovoked invitation, Ben and Sarah exchanged glances, realizing instantly that they were both thinking the same thing. Just two days earlier, when they were sharing a devotion together, they had read the words of Jesus as recorded in Matthew 25:35, "For I was hungry and you gave me something to eat, I was thirsty and you gave me something to drink, I was a stranger and you invited me in, I needed clothes and you clothed me."

Looking now at Fred, they knew what they must do. Fred was no dirty, dangerous stranger, rather he was a needy child of the heavenly Father whom had been guided to a place under a bright star, right into their lives. Ben looked at Sarah, Amy and Martha, all of whom seemed to be pleading with their eyes. He was rewarded with three beautiful smiles as he said, "Yes Fred, we would like you to come celebrate Christmas with us, that is, if you don't have other plans." Sarah touched Fred on the arm and said, "Please do come Mr. Stone. We'd love to have you!"

Amy's high pitched voice chimed in, "Say yes Fwed! Sanna's comin'. Wet's go!" Last, but not least, Martha finally found her voice and looking at Fred with a puppy dog kind of look in her eyes, she almost pleaded, "Please, won't you come celebrate Christmas with us Mr. Stone?"

Fred's eyes filled with tears once more as he looked down and wrung his hands nervously. After a second or two he cleared his throat and uttered, "Oh,... I want to thank you so much, but... but I can't." Ben didn't need to know about Fred's past or to be told that he had experienced some very difficult times. It didn't matter if Fred owned little more than the tattered clothes on his back and whatever was contained within the dirty knapsack hanging at his side. Against Fred's protests of, "No, I can't." Ben and the girls kept insisting that he join them, until his denials became grateful responses of, "Okay, thank you and God bless you!"

Finally, after having given in, and joyfully admitting defeat, or victory, according to how one would choose to view it, Fred added, "I will only come if you all will grant me the honor of one simple request." They all looked at him silently with curiosity written across their faces. Then with a country drawl and a slow smile he added, "Mista' Stone was muh' Father. Ah'd sho' take it kind if'n' ya'all would jest call me Fred." Ben grinned at him and said, "Well then Fred, Let's get going."

Fred let Amy lead him by the hand down the church's aisle and at the back doors, an usher handed them both a bag of Christmas goodies which made their eyes light up with curious wonder. Reaching into the bags, they simultaneously pulled out big candy canes, unwrapped them and stuck them into their mouths. Pastor Miller just winked at Ben as he shook his hand and then he wished each of them a "Merry Christmas," as they donned their coats and descended the church's steps.

Instantly upon stepping out into the refreshingly cold of the night, Ben could see his breath on the air. There was just the right amount of snow on the ground, not enough to be dangerous, but enough to look beautiful. As they made their way across the parking lot Ben kept tossing handful's of snow in the air over Amy's head. She squealed in delight, and he entertained thoughts of doing the same to Sarah until she gave him one of those, "Don't you dare," looks. Beams of light meandered over the frosty landscape from the headlights of departing vehicles adding to the Christmas mystique of the night. The sky was bright with the twinkling of millions of stars surrounding a bright white sliver of a moon and somewhere out in the darkness of night, a dog was barking.

At the car, Ben finally gave into the ever-youthful temptation to toss a handful of loose snow into the air over Sarah's head. Amy laughed gleefully as the sparkling crystals settled all over her mother's head and shoulders, but the look Sarah gave Ben nearly made him want to run to the safety of the opposite side of the parking lot. He was on the verge of begging her forgiveness, when she suddenly broke out into a smile, shaking her head and he knew that everything was okay. Suddenly feeling like a mischievous kid, Ben grabbed another handful of the white powder with the devilish intent to toss it over Sarah's head again, or at least that was until she shook her head and gave him her look of, "I've had enough!" It froze him in his tracks. He then turned his attention to Martha, whom gave him a similar look, but then looking at Fred, he was tickled to see him pointing in Amy's direction again. After another proper aerial powdering, Amy looked more like a laughing angel made of snow than a little girl. Another look from Sarah ended the snow-time fun and after she brushed Amy off, they all got in the car.

Ben started it up and turned the defroster on full blast. Soon a spot large enough to see through materialized on the windshield and they were on their way with Ben, Sarah and Amy, who was busily slurping on her candy cane in the front seat and Martha and Fred, who also was still thoroughly enjoying his peppermint treat, in the back. No one seemed to notice the odor which filled the cars interior emitting from their unwashed guest.

Christmas carols and laughter could be heard emitting from the big, green four-door sedan as it traveled towards the

Chamber's home. They were going to pick up some presents and a little food which Sarah and Martha had prepared and head for Ben's parent's home. They always celebrated Christmas Eve at his folk's, Christmas morning at home and Christmas afternoon with Sarah's family. At the house, Ben, Sarah and Fred got out while Amy stayed in the car with Martha telling her all about the things she hoped Santa Claus would bring her later that night. Sarah disappeared into the house and Ben was about to follow her, when he realized that Fred was nervously trying to muster up the gumption to say something to him.

"What is it Fred," Ben asked as he turned and paused on the front porch steps. Fred stared down silently at his feet for a moment and then as if mustering up some courage he raised his head and looked Ben square in the eyes with a despondent and painful look. Clearing his throat and stumbling for words he said, "B... Ben? I really appreciate ya'all bringin' me along, but I,... I can't, ya' know, I can't go with ya'. Not like this....!" He looked down, obviously ashamed by his appearance and Ben became acutely aware once again, at just how bad of shape his new friend was in. Then, Ben smiled gently because he had the answer for Fred's current predicament. Putting a hand on Fred's shoulder he said, "Don't you worry about a thing Brother, I've got just what you need. Sarah and the girls can go on to my parent's home and we'll take the truck and meet up with them in a short while." Fred smiled back at Ben as Sarah came through the door with her arms full. She looked at Ben as if to say, "Why are you still standing out here," but she actually said, "Honey, I could use a little help here." Then Fred and Ben helped Sarah unload what she was carrying into the car's trunk. After three more trips into the house they had everything ready to go.

Then Ben explained to Sarah what he had in mind and she was in total agreement. He walked over and opened the driver's side door for her, gave her a quick kiss and let Amy and Martha know what was going on. As Sarah started to pull out of the drive, Ben quickly reached down for a hand full of snow, packed it tightly into a ball and threw it at the side window of the car when he saw Amy and Martha both peering out, taunting him. They had their tongues stuck out and their hands spread with their thumbs in their ears making moose antlers. As the snowball burst into a million ice crystals and slid down the window they burst into laughter and Sarah pulled away. As the taillights disappeared down the road Ben walked back up to the porch, where Fred was standing with a smile on his face. "You're a bit on the ornery side, ain't ya' Ben?" Ben rubbed his hands together, knocking off the residual snow and replied, "Not as a practice my new friend, but rest assured and watch out, for I do have my unpredictable moments." Then he clapped Fred on the back and said, "Well Buddy, let's see about getting you cleaned up a bit," and they went into the house.

CHAPTER FOUR

The heat in the house felt good, and the sweet scent of pine lingered in the air, as Ben removed his coat. He looked at Fred whom was staring silently, as if transfixed, at the family's Christmas tree, which was decorated and lit just inside the living room window. A few random presents lay atop a plaid tree skirt, but that would change sometime in the wee hours of the night of course, after Santa came. As he walked up next to his unkempt guest he became increasingly aware of the awful nauseating odor of a long unwashed body permeating the living room, and he felt sorry for him. Ben wondered, "What thoughts must be going through his mind? What is his story and just who is he, really? Does he have any family and what led him here?"

"Do you want something to drink Fred, some coffee, cocoa, tea or anything," Ben asked. Jerking as if startled, Fred turned towards Ben looking scared and confused for a slight instance, as if he had forgotten where he was. Almost immediately however, recognition filtered into his eyes and he smiled at his host and drawled in his uniquely deep tone, "Ah don't wanna be a bother to ya' Ben, but a spot o' wakey juice sho' sounds like necta' from God, ta' me." Ben couldn't help but laugh as he said, "Wakey juice? I surely can't say as I've ever heard of that before. What is it?" With a glint of humor in his eyes, Fred replied, "Awww' come on Ben, don't ya' know? Ah' be referin' ta' a servin' of bean juice, a spot of brew, a cup of joe, java, mawnin' thunder... ?"

Ben quickly put his hands up in the air with a feigned look of disgust due to insult and exclaimed, "Alright already, I get it! I'm not stupid, you know! You want a cup of coffee! Why didn't you just say so?" Starting to chuckle, Fred backed up a step, put his own hands up and replied, "Simmer down, a bit, ah sho don't want ya ta' hev a coronary on Christmas Eve." Then in a mocking, but seriously, deep and suddenly cultured voice he added, "Mr. Chamber's, Sir, perhaps if you would not mind, I would most definitely be inclined to graciously accept your kind offer of some dry roast. Simply black, if you please."

Although he was nigh on to splitting a gut inside, Ben contained his laughter, still donning his own version of a serious look as he responded, "Well, that's better, but this isn't one of those fancy, city-slicker, foo-foo joints. All we have here is plain old, ordinary coffee. Where in the world did you come up with a name like, 'Wakey Juice' anyway?" Still smiling, Fred answered, "Ah' reckon I started callin' coffee that in the Army while I was o'er there, in... in, Nam,... ya know?" Fred's smile slowly faded as he said this and his eyes looked a bit troubled, as if a sudden sad memory had come to the surface. "You were over there," Ben asked. Fred slowly nodded, but offered no further comment and Ben felt like he had inadvertently hit a sore spot.

Ben himself had been in the Army also and he had spent his fair share of time in Vietnam. He and his old Army buddies seldom talked about it, but when they did, they still had nightmares and their stories usually left their listeners stunned and at a loss for words. Some veterans had returned okay, some changed and many had not returned at all. Ben knew from experience that sometimes the worst scars are the ones you cannot see. He had several hidden away inside of himself as a result of his time, over there. Fred had obviously returned from the war, but Ben wondered how many hidden battle scars, whether they be physical, mental or emotional, he might still be carrying with him.

"So, you were over there, huh? Me too, Buddy. I'm sure glad that horrible chapter of my life is over, aren't you," Ben added. Fred slowly nodded, but said nothing and Ben took that as a subtle hint to change the subject to something more pleasant. Putting on his best "welcome" smile he said, "Come along with me Fred, and I'll show you the house and to your room." Still wearing his tattered Army jacket and carrying the dirty knapsack, Fred meekly followed Ben from room to room and then to the guest bedroom at the end of the hall. Ben became increasingly aware that Fred must have wanted to say something, but was having trouble finding the words. He thought he knew what it was, and carefully, so as not to offend his guest he asked, "Fred, would you like to spruce up a little before we join the girls at my folk's house?" Fred hung his head, appearing as if he were a little ashamed and nodded slowly. Pointing to the soiled bag hanging loosely at Fred's side, Ben asked, "Do you have a change of clothes in there?" Fred looked up sadly into Ben's eyes as he indicated that he did not with a embarrassed shake of his scraggly head. With his heart going out to this poor man standing before him, Ben said, "Fred my friend, don't you worry about a thing. Reach into that there bag of yours and find your smile, because I should have everything else you need. So tell me, what size of clothes you wear?"

As Fred rumbled off the sizes, Ben was once more surprised. Isn't it just like God to lead a needy stranger to the door of someone who wears nearly the same size of clothing and the exact same size shoe, as they themselves do? "Fred, leave your bag here and follow me," Ben exclaimed.

Fred sat his bag on the bed and followed Ben once more. In his bedroom, Ben dug out a couple of brand new pairs of socks and underwear, still in their packages, which he had received for his birthday a month earlier. He found a nice pair of blue jeans, an extra belt and from off of a hanger in the closet, he grabbed a sweater that he seldom wore anyway. He found an extra pair of brown dress shoes which were slightly worn, but he was sure that Fred wouldn't mind. Then he showed him where the bathroom, towels and toiletries were and at Fred's request, he produced a pair of electric trimmers, a razor, toothbrush and shaving foam. Ben even threw in a small bottle of aftershave he suddenly remembered was hiding in the back of his sock drawer since last Christmas. Then he left Fred and went into the kitchen to brew up some coffee.

Soon, the hum of trimmers reverberated from down the hall. By the time that the aromatic splendor of coffee was drifting through the house, Ben could hear the shower running. As he waited, he utilized the time by getting Sarah's Christmas presents out of hiding and put them under the tree. This year, he had successfully hidden some of them, or so he thought, atop the pull-down stairway access to the attic. Sarah was a "peeker," who had never been able to resist curiosity when it came to presents.

Although she did discover the stairway hiding place one day, she never had the opportunity to peel back the wrapped ends this year. She did however, find a few other hidden gifts throughout the house. Knowing Sarah's weakness always influenced Ben to indulge in a temptation of his own each year. In order to get one over on her, he always wrapped a few bizarre items for her to find. This year it had been a mummified mouse he found in the garage one day and a small box of broken drill bits.

Ben had nearly rolled on the floor in laughter on the day Sarah came shrieking into the living room, when she discovered the mouse. He had hidden it in a place that wasn't too obvious, but where she would be sure to find it, in one of her old purses. He had been waiting for over a week for her to discover it. So great was her terror when she finally did, that she got Amy to start crying as well. Ben laughter was swallowed in a quick nervous gulp. When yet another version of "The look," glared at him from Sarah's suddenly enraged eyes. The next day, she could laugh about the incident as well, and reluctantly concede that Ben was indeed, the "Master Jokester", but at the moment, she found no humor in the strategically placed, prank gift. Needless to say however, it didn't diminish her desire to continue searching for other of her presents. She never did find the drill bits though and Ben forgot about them until nearly two years later when Amy stumbled across them one day in the back of the hallway closet.

Ben heard the water shut off from down the hall and after a few minutes the bathroom door squeaked open and footsteps on the hall's hardwood floor echoed from down the hall. Then the guest bedroom door closed. He couldn't help but wonder what Fred was going to look like when he came out. Before going into the bathroom, he appeared to be a pretty rough character, but never once did Ben doubt that by taking Fred in this evening, he and his family were doing the right thing. He was convinced that it was what God wanted them to do. After all, it was Christmas Eve, the night of giving. He went to the kitchen and poured two cups of coffee, putting both cream and sugar in his own. Earlier in the day, Sarah had baked some chocolate chip cookies, some to take to his parent's this evening and the rest for enjoying at home. Ben was putting a few of these on a napkins, when he heard someone step into the kitchen behind him. "Your timing is perfect, Fred. I hope you like fresh, homemade cookies with your coffee," he said.

Ben didn't know what to expect when he turned around, but when he did, he was even more surprised than he had been when a certain dirty, smelly stranger had sat next to him in church about an hour ago. There before him, stood a man, completely transformed from someone you would have found yourself tempted to back away from, into a clean cut, smiling gentleman known as Mr. Frederick F. Stone. Ben couldn't help but notice that Fred looked better in that old sweater than he ever had and all he could say was, "Whoa! Where's Fred? You really know how to clean up, Pal." Smelling of soap and aftershave, with his cheeks red from razor burn, Fred just smiled. No one would have believed he was the same man who had worn the old Army Jacket.

Gone was the long scraggly hair, the beard, the filthy tattered clothing and the mismatched shoes. The layers of dirt and grime had been washed away and judging by the sparkle in his eyes, so too removed, had been a heavy load from his shoulders, one full of stress, sorrow, frustration and grief. Ben knew that he could claim a little credit for the physical transformation which had taken place, but only God alone could be held accountable for the smile now plastered across Fred's face and the newfound joy within his heart.

Ben smiled from his recliner as he reminisced over that Christmas Eve night in 1972. Sarah walked into the room smelling like perfume and vanilla bath wash and sat on the armrest of his chair. She kissed him gently and then taking his hand she said, "You must be feeling a little better Dear. What are you smiling about?" Ben squeezed her hand and replied, "I was just thinking about when we first met Fred and how he looked and the difference after he got himself all cleaned up. Do you remember that night, back when Amy was only four years old?" Sarah smiled and replied, "Of course I remember. How could I forget? When you guys got to your parent's house, he was nearly as handsome as you were, and poor Martha, she spilled her iced tea all over herself when she saw him walk into the room. Ben laughed as he remembered and then he added, "Those two surely didn't let any grass grow under their feet, did they?" Sarah shook her head with a smile and rubbed Ben's shoulder as she answered, "No, they sure didn't. It definitely was a case of love at first sight."

For a few moments, the pain of the last few days was gone until Ben once again, remembered the accident. "It's just not fair Honey! It wasn't his time! He was younger than I am, and poor Martha, what is she going to do now? They didn't even have any kids, so there's no one here for her now, except us. I wish, I... I just wish... how could God let this hap... ?" Sarah had to brush away a tear as she hugged Ben tightly and said, "Oh Ben, shhhhhh! God didn't choose for this to happen, it just did. We just have to believe that everything is going to be okay. Come on, let's go pray and try to get some sleep, okay?" Ben knew that Sarah was right, but at the moment he didn't want to pray or go to sleep. What he really wanted to do was to go outside and yell at the top of his voice to Heaven and give God a fair piece of his mind. Even just the thought of doing such a thing secretly shamed Ben inside his heart, but inside he was hurting and furious. He wanted, needed, actually had to blame someone.

Sarah, with a soft and soothing voice, talked some sensibility back into him and soon they were walking down the hall, hand in hand to check on Sammi. She was sleeping soundly and just the sight of her angelic features and the gentle sound of her steady breathing calmed Ben down. Once in bed, he and Sarah read a daily devotion together and prayed. After switching off the lamp next to the bed and kissing Sarah good night, Ben lay awake thinking. It wasn't too long before Sarah's steady snoring signified to Ben, that she too, had joined Sammi in slumber land. Ben forced himself to remember the good times they had spent with Fred and eventually, he too drifted off to sleep somewhere deep in the middle of the night.

About one hundred yards away, Martha too was struggling against painful emotions and trying to fall asleep. The bed felt so cold and empty, just like her heart and she had cried more times this evening than she could count. Her sorrow was the greatest she has known since losing her parents and she couldn't decide if she was mad at God or needed him more than ever now. In desperation she had searched the pages of her Bible to find some kind of answer or comfort for her pain, but twice she ended up sending it sailing across the room in frustration. Each time, she felt as though she had committed some great sin and ran to pick it up, crying and asking God to forgive her, to make her faith stronger and to simply just give her the strength to make it through the night. "Oh God! I miss you Freddy, I miss you so much!... It's not fair," she cried over and over.

It had only been four days since the accident and yesterday they had laid his body to rest. It still didn't seem like it could possibly be real, and Martha kept praying that she would just wake up and discover that it all had been one horrendous nightmare. She wanted so desperately for Fred to come walking into the door and to hear his deep voice tell her that he loved her, but the undeniable pain in her chest, let her know that this was no dream, it was cold, hard reality and Fred was really gone. Her faith told her that he was in Heaven, he was okay and that some day she would see him again, but right now, some day, seemed like forever away. As she sat up in her bed with the "Good Book" in her lap, she didn't know what to do. Ben and Sarah had tried everything they could to help, but there are some wounds that friends just cannot heal. Martha flipped open her Bible and stuck her finger on a page hoping to miraculously discover a verse that would heal her hurt. The verse was Psalms 34:18, "The Lord is close to the brokenhearted and saves those crushed in spirit." When she read the verse she let out a hysterical laugh and anger flashed through her mind as she sarcastically said aloud, "Lord! What about those crushed in accidents?"

Immediately she started crying, asking God to forgive her anger-fueled sarcasm. When she looked down again at her Bible, she discovered that the pages had fanned shut all of the way to the book of Matthew. Chapter 28, verse 20b. seemed to shine up at her. It read, "And surely I am with you always, to the very end of the age." A warm sensation settled over Martha as she slowly closed the Bible and laid it on her night stand. She switched off the lamp and lay in the darkness thinking about those words, "Surely I am with you always." and she pictured Fred's smiling face. She longed to touch him, to smell him and to hear his snoring beside her. She wanted to feel his arms wrapped tightly around her and to hold his hand everywhere they went. She loved that lost puppy dog look he got when he messed things up and the glint in his eye when he had just pulled a good prank on someone. "God, please help me! I just want my best friend," she cried softly. Slowly her grief gave way to happier memories and she could hear Fred's deep, deep voice talking to her. It said, "I will always be with you Dear! I love you Martha!" Martha smiled softly in the darkness and murmured, "I love you too Freddy!" as she slowly drifted off to sleep, mercifully escaping her heart-broke misery, even if, for only a few hours.

Outside, the eerie yipping of coyotes on the run echoed across the fields. A hoot owl issued forth his mournful serenade into the cool darkness from the very same spot, on the power lines in front of Ben and Sarah's house, which the hungry hawk had occupied earlier in the day. A car passed by on the road under the power lines and the owl took off on silent wings, drifting into the ebony shadows of the night in search of an easily gotten late night meal. The flashing lights of several jets, passing high over head seemed to inch across the sky like slow moving caterpillars and a tomcat scrambled noisily out of one of Ben's garbage cans, carrying off a small piece of fried chicken. A large gray opossum feasted on apples beneath Ben's apple tree and the big spider in the tire swing repaired and strengthened his webbed creation. The harmony of crickets and the occasional input of a tree frog blended with the fading drone of a motorcycle. The hushed whisper of rustling leaves stirring in a gentle breeze and something was walking out in the field near the house. Moths and an occasional brown bat darted about in the glow of Ben's yard light and across the street, the lights went out in a neighbors house.

Beneath a starlit sky with the moon shining bright, all of this, and yet, so very much more, brings to a close, another day. Despite the recent tragedy which has occurred, the whole world seems at peace. The sting of death and the pains of mourning are held at bay as life continues to do simply that which it does best, what it must,... it goes on.

CHAPTER FIVE

Seconds turn into minutes, minutes into hours and hours blend into days. The chronicles of time continue to march onward despite the hardships we face. Sometimes when we seem to be at the lowest point of our lives, people often try to uplift us by saying, "Better days are in store, just you wait and see." At the time, we really don't want to hear that, or for that matter, we don't wish to subscribe to any seemingly, empty promises of future happiness. Maybe, it's because we are mad, or at least for the moment, we really don't believe it to be possible, although deep inside we actually know it is true. Part of us wants those better days to get here in a hurry, but at the same time, another unexplainable part of us wants to hang on to our anger, misery, and pain. We want to blame someone and we want some kind of justice. Perhaps we subconsciously fear that if we let go of the bad and focus on feeling good again, that we will forget, that person or thing we have lost, which was so important to us in the first place. We need not fret however, for that will never happen. The good things in life and the people we have loved, stay in our hearts and our memories forever.

Ben was finding out, even if he wasn't aware of it, that he is one of those people who doesn't really believe that time heals all wounds or at least not quickly enough. He wants answers and some form of closure. He not only wants to believe, but he also wants to actually feel, that somehow, everything is alright. Sadly for him however, he still only feels the pain it isn't alright. Fred is still gone and Ben is not ready to say that it is okay. Time has passed on as it always does. Before anyone stopped to give it any thought, "Trick or Treat" had come and gone, Thanksgiving has passed on, and it is now the early morning hours of Christmas Eve, 2006. Nearly everywhere in Ben's community, decorations announce the yuletide event, many bringing honor and praise to Christ the Newborn King, while yet others are completely commercialized and directed at a totally different message. Nativity scenes, stars, banners, and angels mingle with lighted trees, holographic projections, plywood cutouts, plastic Santa's, snowmen, reindeer, and symbols reminiscent of a more secular Christmas. Lighted decorations hang from each "Main Street" light pole in town and every business storefront window announces the upcoming holiday in its own unique fashion.

Over the last few days, children of all ages have been excited because school is out and a great time of joy is quickly approaching. They have been feasting on home-made cookies, singing Christmas carols and dreaming about what wonderful gifts they hoped to soon be giving and receiving. The desire for snow, fills the minds of many would-be young sled riders and snow creation constructors. Adults here and there, like usual are filled with worry. They are anxiously concerned with money, sickness, getting the perfect gifts, having the best decorated yard and most anything you can think of, but they too, are trying to kindle their Christmas fires and get into the spirit of the season. The bell ringers have graced the fronts of stores for several weeks and an epidemic of giving has swept the area. The Christmas tree lot on West 4th St. is nearly empty and Santa's house in the square has received more visitors than ever before, this year. One of those wide-eyed visitors was little Sammi. Ben took her there just a few days ago and for five bucks, he got a so-so quality instant picture of her sitting on the jolly man's lap. Sammi was too busy smiling to notice the edge of the pillow sticking out beneath the red cloak or the yellowed edges of the fake beard. All she knew was, "That bearded man in the red suit was Santa, he had candy, and she was going to get a lot of presents from him for she had been a good girl all year."

Even amidst his secret despair, Ben has found his smiles to be genuine in the presence of Sammi. He loves her so much that he cannot help himself, especially with her so aglow with Christmas anticipation. This year, she is going to be an angel in the Christmas Eve program at the church, just as her mother, Amy, had been years ago, but neither of them had to dress up to be an angel in Ben's eyes.

Sarah has been caught up in the Christmas season for several weeks, actually since shopping on the big sale day, the renowned day after Thanksgiving. Ben has really been trying to share in her exhilleration, and although he outwardly has appeared to be full of the seasonal joy, she realizes that on the inside, he is still desperately struggling with what happened to Fred. Martha too, has been doing her best to join in the Christmas-time celebration, spending nearly every day with Sarah, shopping, baking, wrapping presents and even caroling down at the local senior center.

When people asked her how she is doing, she flashes a bright smile and replies, "Oh, praise the Lord! I'm doing just fine!" It is a good ruse and sometimes she even convinced herself that it was true, but Ben and Sarah are both very worried about her. They can always detect that wistful look, lurking deep inside of her eyes and they each painfully know that she was hurting something fierce inside. Ben knows, that just like him, she still wants and desperately needs, answers. She longs for everything to be okay, like it was before, but how can it be, when before, is no more? Financially she is doing okay, but this year, understandably so, Christmas is having difficulty in getting a response from its knock at her hearts door.

Each day lately, when he prays, Ben has been asking God for some sense of closure for both Martha and himself. Ben has always believed that God answers our prayers with either a "Yes", a "No" or a "Wait," but lately he fears that maybe God has went on vacation. The answer had not yet arrived. Ben is not willing to accept a "No." response and if it were a case of waiting, he felt as though they has waited far too long already. Many times recently, Ben has reminded himself also to never again pray for patience because ironically, God will often give you what you ask for. In the case of "patience", the process of learning it is usually much more stressful and difficult than any sane individual would want to go through.

Sometimes when he prays, Ben imagines that Fred is looking down upon him and listening. This makes him wish all the more that his friend was still standing beside him. On the day of Fred's funeral, he promised that he and Sarah would always look after Martha, and if they ever understood why Fred had been taken from them, they would also try to help her to understand it. They have prayed about it so many times that Ben half believes that maybe God is tired of hearing about it, but he continues to pray anyway. Today on this new Christmas Eve, sometime before it comes to a close, all of their prayers are once again going to be answered in unique fashion.

CHAPTER SIX

B en awoke to the distant sound of a train's whistle echoing across the countryside. Just moments earlier, he had been dreaming, of what, he had no recollection. He could hear Sarah's steady breathing beside him and he slid carefully out of the bed so as to not awaken her. A quick glance at the electric rooster beside the bed informed him that it was nearly 6:00 a.m. and it was still dark outside. Aside from the sound of Sarah sleeping, it was strangely quiet in the house. Ben softly made his way to the bathroom and then to the kitchen where he made some hot chocolate in the microwave. Looking out the back window, he could see by the glow of the yard light that it had snowed more than just a little over night. Even in the partial darkness it was beautiful to behold and Ben didn't mind at all that his backyard now appeared a winter wonderland. The children would be happy to play in it and in a way, so too was Ben. For the first time in many weeks he smiled a real smile that wasn't inspired by Sammi.

Ben had a truck with a blade attachment on the front and today, he was going to get to push some snow. Thinking about it made him feel like a kid again. He walked into the living room with his hot chocolate, sipping the little marshmallows off of the top. He breathed in deep, savoring the rich, sweet aroma as he walked over to the Christmas tree. He plugged in the lights, noticing how beautifully decorated the tree was this year. He and Sammi had helped Sarah to decorate it the weekend after Thanksgiving, but it was like he was seeing it for the first time. The rest of the room was dark, but the strings of lights on the tree made its ornaments glisten and sparkle like gem stones in a jewelers case. As he glanced from one ornament to the next, he noticed that one of them was hanging crooked. Reaching out, he adjusted the ornament, sighing as he did so, for once again, his thoughts were back on Fred.

Fred had always insisted that every Christmas tree absolutely must be decorated with utmost perfection and each ornament had to be straight. Thinking back, Ben pictured Fred straightening a crooked ornament and he could almost hear his deep voice saying, "Dis' tree needs ta' be jest right fer' Jesus! Crook'd hanging's won't do." Fred didn't just believe that the ornaments had to be right, but the star atop the tree, and oh yes, it had to be a star, it had to be perfectly straight as well. Ben chuckled a bit as he recalled how Martha used to toy with Fred, by tilting the star to one side or the other. She would pretend to be 'plumb and level' challenged, until Fred would belt out in his gentle thunder-like voice, "Woman, yer' eyes must be set crook'd!" Then he'd stand on his tip-toes reaching over Martha, straighten the star and then wrap his arms around her and say, "Thar' Dear, now it's jest' right!"

Martha always smiled at that point, feeling warm, safe and secure in his loving embrace and she'd say with a smile, "Yes, it surely is!" They re-enacted this little routine every Christmas and it never got old. When Ben and Sarah got the opportunity to see it, they were usually moved to hug one another also. "Martha is sure going to miss those hugs," Ben thought sadly as he walked over and sunk into his recliner. He finished his cocoa, sat the cup on the end table and sighed again. His heart started pounding hard in his chest and suddenly a wave of despair washed over him once more, just as it had so many times since that awful day when Fred went away. Tears welled up in Ben's eyes and he leaned back in his recliner, staring upward, gazing not at the ceiling, but far beyond to God in Heaven. Silently, but with tormented anguish, he pleaded, "Oh my God, please,... won't you please help me! The pain is supposed to get easier with time! I'm supposed to get used to it, aren't I? I can barely stand it! Why?... Why won't you help me?"

Although it had been over two months now, Ben was no more used to Fred's sudden departure than he had been the day it occurred. He had absolutely no idea how Martha was surviving, because he was barely making it himself. Every day he missed his old friend more and more. Nearly everything reminded him of Fred in one way or another and the pain of saying, "Good bye." was always just a thought away. Ben was even starting to worry, that perhaps Fred's dying the way he had was causing him to lose his own faith. It wasn't even so much the dying as it was anger, resulting from the lack of answers, at least any which made sense. It just seemed so unfair.

Finally, Ben's eyes stopped watering and he somewhat got control of his emotions. On the wall across the room from Ben, just to the left of the Christmas tree and between the picture window and door hung a picture which drew his attention. In the dim glow cast by the Christmas tree lights, he could barely see it, but he knew the picture so well that it was sharp and clear in his mind. It was a picture of Martha and Sarah sitting in chairs with Fred and Ben standing behind them and Sammi laying across the women's laps. They had the photo shot one day, during a special sale, going on at a department store at the mall. The sixteen by twenty photograph showed everyone flashing a tooth-filled smile, or almost. Everyone that is, except for the fact that Fred's smile had a very noticeable black gap, where his upper, left incisor should have been. He had went around that way for several months before getting some work done at the dentist.

As Ben visualized Fred's hapless smile, he remembered the day when Sammi first noticed the missing tooth and asked him about it. She was almost three years old and very much like now, she was constantly full of inquisitive questions. The thing was however, you never knew what she might ask. That day had had been one full of fun at the County Fair. Sarah and Martha were volunteering a two-hour shift at the church's food booth while Sammi, Fred and Ben were busy feasting on once-a-year delicacies like cotton candy, funnel cake and orange shake-ups while checking out tractors and the live stock exhibits. When they got half way through the cattle barn, Sammi noticed a pile of straw bales stacked three high. Instantly, she tugged on Ben's hand, steering him towards them saying, "Up PamPaw! Wift me up! Pwease!" She squealed with delight as Ben scooped her up and stood her on the bales. Fred walked up to the edge of the bales and teased her saying, "Yer' as tall as me now, Kiddo!" Sammi just giggled, staring at him face to face for a moment, but then she suddenly got a serious look on her face. It was as if she were seeing him for the first time. When he asked her what was wrong, her response nearly caused Ben to roll on the ground laughing. With sincere concern in her voice and her eyes big like a innocent newborn fawn's, she asked, "Fwed, what happen to yo' tooth? Did yo fogit' ta' bwush?"

Fred smiled at her for a second and then stuck the tip of his tongue through the gap at Sammi, eliciting a laugh from both she and Ben. Then he replied, "Well Sammi, ah' guess ya' could say thet' ah forgot to switch on muh' radar one night." He went on to explain how one night, just after he and Martha had went to bed and pulled up the covers that he remembered he had forgotten to turn off the garage light. As he got up out of bed, he couldn't see a thing because his eyes weren't adjusted to the dark yet. Unbeknownst to Fred, the bedroom's door had swung half way shut when he came into the room, and as fate would have it, poor Fred ended up running smack dab, right into the edge of the door splitting his lip and knocking out his tooth. By the time he found the light switch, the blood was flowing and Martha nearly freaked out at the sight of him.

First thing in the morning, they went to see their dentist, but it was several months before Fred got the new gap in his smile filled in. Anytime Fred caught a bit of ribbing over his toothless smile, he'd just poke the tip of his tongue through the gap and boldly say to his would-be tormentors, "It's da' Lord's way of keepin' ole' Fred humble, cuz' of muh' good looks, ya know!" Even now from his recliner, Ben couldn't help but to marvel at how Fred had always possessed a a unique sense of optimism, with which to face everything in his life. He thought about Fred's faith and his attitude and then gazing heavenward once more he softly asked, "Lord, what would Fred think about you calling him home, before his time?" After a minute of silence and sensing no answer Ben's impatient anger reared it's ugly head for just a moment, until in his mind, he started to relive the events of that tragic day. He hated going where his memories were leading him, but he felt helpless to resist. He wished that he could go back and change things or do something,... anything that could bring Fred back. Warm, salty tears ran down Ben's face and across his trembling lips as a familiar pain came from deep within. He grasped the armrest of his recliner, looked up towards the Christmas tree's star without really seeing it and muttered, "Anything Lord,... is there anything I can do?... Anything at all?"

The living room slowly faded into oblivion and soon, Ben's mind traveled back in time, not a long ways, but to a hard time. It even seemed worse than Vietnam, because even there, he still had hope for better days. Ben squirmed in his chair, not wanting to mentally relive that which was perhaps, the most difficult of his life. Sure, presently it was Christmas Eve morning the day of great joy, and it had snowed. Outside, the eastern sky was just started to brighten with the promise of sunshine, but Ben didn't notice the glow coming through the window behind the Christmas tree. For the moment, he didn't care about yuletide spirit, the snow that would be sparkling like diamonds in the bright sunlight or the fun he would have pushing it with his blade. In fact, Ben's mind wasn't even cognizant of Winter for his focus was riveted onto a particularly painful Fall day. It was a day that started out with the greatest of promise for fun and adventure, yet it took a devastating left turn which ended up in misery. In his thoughts, today wasn't the day of insurmountable joy, Christmas Eve. Rather, it was seemingly forever, that awful day when the world relinquished one of its best and Ben, lost not only his best friend, but also a huge part of himself. It was very early in the morning, and Ben would not have even gotten out of bed, if he had only known what was in store for that day. It was,... the 29th of September.

CHAPTER SEVEN

"Whooooeeee!... She's a big un', Ben ole' boy. Keep yer' line tawt' n' reel er' in!" Fred's deep voice boomed over the still waters, scaring two deer which had come to the ponds edge for an early dawn's drink. A mourning dove on the shore took off with a shrill call in a flurry of feathers as if fearing that a giant was soon to attack. A muskrat swimming near the aluminum john-boat disappeared, diving into the depths of the green, murky, unknown and a startled turtle slid into the refreshingly cool water from the rock near the cattails, where he had been sunning himself. Fred's thunderous exclamations continued, "Yer a reelin' too fast Buddy!... Keep yer' pole up, and...an'..." He was intentionally cut off by Ben's snappy reply of, "I've got it Mr. Pro-Fish-ional! Don't have yourself a coronary, it ain't my first time to the dance, you know!" Then with a quick grin at his fishing buddy, he added, "She sure does feel like a whale. Get that net ready, okay?"

It's hard to say who was more excited of the two men, but when that monster of a large-mouth bass broke the surface in a spray of water, both of their hearts nearly leapt out of their chests. When Ben got the fighting fish within twenty feet of the boat, it flew up out of the water again. Suddenly, for just the slightest of moments, time seemed to stand still and it puzzled Ben. Fred still hollering excitedly right across from him in the small boat, but it was as if he were far away and his words never reached Ben's ears. He shook off his curiosity and looked back to where his rod's string entered the lake. As the diving bass left the water again, it drew Ben's attention in the weirdest of ways. It wasn't as an angler or even an adversary. Rather, it was strangely as if through a weird, small chain of unusual events, the fish's purpose in getting hooked on his line was to tell him something of the utmost importance. In the sunlight, the under-belly of the fish appeared as a brilliant flash of white and the drops of water spraying all around it looked like diamonds. Amidst the cascading, sparkling drops, dragonflies darted about, strangely appearing to Ben, as if they were somehow, royal servants heralding the upcoming important message of a king. Confusion clouded his mind as the long, thin, green bodies of the dragonflies seemed to disappear and the jade hued side of the bass appeared before him close enough to touch. Time seemed to slow down even more, nearly to a standstill.

He could see the smooth, supple muscles of the fish's body moving and twitching beneath his colorful scales. The spinner bait on Ben's line was barely visible in the huge open mouth of the fish. Films of moisture seemed to slowly draw together into drops which subsequently flew into the open air. The bass's fins were rigid and it must have weighed over twelve pounds, but it wasn't the impressive size of the lake denizen that captivated Ben the most, it was its eyes, or specifically, the eye which was now looking straight at him. He became acutely aware of nothing more than gazing into the fish's eye. At first it appeared to be of normal size, white, with a black pupil and blank as if it were a creature with no thought or emotion, but instantly it changed. The eye seemed to expand and the pupil took on an unexplain-able glint of mysterious light. It was like getting a glimpse into some unknown form of intelligence blended with an all-knowing sense of being alive. Suddenly, even though its physically impos-sible, the great fish blinked at him and from out of the blue he heard little Sammi's sweet, innocent voice say with complete confidence, "Don't worry PamPaw, Jesus told me, evwythin' will be all-wight'!" Then time went back to normal, the diving fish disappeared once more into the water and Ben could hear

Fred's deep voice hollering, "Ya' jest about got er' Ben! Reel er' in easy like."

Sure it sounds crazy. After all, Fred and Ben were alone in the boat and time doesn't really go into slo-mo. Big-mouth bass surely can't blink and Sammi wasn't even there, but that's still what happened. The whole episode, probably didn't last more than a second or two and Ben wasn't even truly aware that it had occurred until later, when he would relive that day, again and again in his thoughts and dreams. As for now however, the excitement of reeling in a big-one, returned and he was loving every minute of it.

Ben held back on the rod and carefully reeled in his prize, anxiously trying not to over do it and break the line. Fred had laid his own gear aside and was eagerly awaiting and ready with the net. The boat was rocking to and fro with the movements of the two avid anglers. They focused their attentions on the taught line drawing closer and closer to the boat as Ben reeled away. Judging by the angle, the bass had to be directly beneath the boat now. Ben gently, but firmly reared back on his rod, praying that the line wouldn't break under the strain of the heavy, live-load fighting under the waters surface. "Hot diggity!... Thar' she be," Fred shouted as he leaned over the side of the boat, scooping into the water with the net. Ben felt the release of tension on his line as Fred had to use both hands to haul in the monstrous, squirming fish. He had caught a few big ones before, but each time, it always felt like the first time. He entertained visions for a moment of his latest catch mounted on the wall above the fireplace in his living room, and his picture up on the wall down at "Lawson's Deli" in town, but as usual, this idea faded into oblivion as he watched Fred's smiling face.

Fred couldn't have been more excited if he had reeled in the fish himself, but Ben knew what was coming. Oh, both men and their wives loved fish at the supper table and occasionally Ben kept a few for that purpose, but ole' Fred, bless his soul, was as soft-hearted as they come. Most fishermen though that he was too strong of a proponent of Catch-and-Release, for he never kept anything he caught. He'd always say, "All God's critters, gots' a rawt' to live, ceptin' skeeters, ticks an such!'' Ben ribbed him relentlessly on occasion about his eating, because you'd better believe, that Fred loved his meat and potatoes. He could wolf down so much burger, steak, chicken or what not, into that thin little body of his, that where it went, was a mystery to all mankind. For every humorous and sometimes sarcastic accusation Ben might throw at Fred for being such a softy, yet an obvious carnivore, he always had a unique comeback that could get you thinking. If the comeback weren't enough to diffuse the intent of the would-be antagonist, then Fred would simply avert the subject.

Many were the times when Fred had been so convincing in his arguments that Ben too, although he would never admit it aloud, felt guilty and would throw back his own catch. He had already silently conceded that today was one of those times, but he wasn't going to give in too easy, however. His eyes sparkled with mischief as he took on a tone of voice that he hoped would not give away his devilish intentions.

"How much does she weigh, Fred?" Ben asked. By now, Fred had taken the bass out of the net, removed the lure and was preparing to put it in the homemade live-well situated between the seats of the boat. "Ah says, bout ne'r on ta' thirteen or so." Fred drawled still grinning as he looked over the fish with admiring eyes. Ben feigned insult as he exclaimed, "What do you mean, thirteen pounds? Open your eyes partner! Can't you see that she's at least fifteen? Why it'll darn near fill up the well. Get that scale behind you and check her out. Thirteen pounds... I never!" Ben was laying it on thick and he couldn't tell for sure if Fred was taking the bait or not. He knew he would soon for sure, though.

After carefully weighing the fish, Fred got a triumphant gleam to his eyes as he pointed at the fish scale, looked at Ben and exclaimed, "Thirteen an' fo' ounces. See! Ah's sho' did tell ya'! Ah was rawt, Ben and thet would make ya wro... ?" Ben cut his friend off, seizing the opportunity he had been looking for as he blurted out with a bit of fake enthusiastic sarcasm, "That there fish would make one mighty fine wall mounting back at the house." Fred's smile slowly disappeared and he stared silently at him for a few seconds. Ben knew that he was thinking hard, trying to figure out if he were talking for real or if it were a joke. Quickly, before he'd crack a smile and ruin the moment, Ben added in as serious of a tone as he could muster, "I can't wait to show this one to everyone, especially Sammi! Maybe she'll want it in her room?" Ben felt his own personal surge of comedic triumph when Fred suddenly bought the whole ruse, hook, line, and sinker.

Poor, poor soft-hearted Fred. He took on a lost puppy dog look, lost his usual country drawl and pleaded very seriously, "Ben Chambers, you cannot possibly mean such a thing? Look at this magnificent fish! (He held the fish up to Ben.) She's a thing of beauty, one of God's precious creatures, why, why... I ought to...! What gives you the right to hang her on your wall? She's lived entirely too long and earned the right to keep on living and...!"

Fred's voice had gotten even deeper, his eyes were bugging and he even had a vein standing out on his neck. He was so serious, yet Ben found the whole ordeal so hilarious that he could no longer contain himself and he nearly fell out of the boat laughing at his hopelessly, gullible friend. Fred slowly calmed down, realizing that he'd been had, and he hung his head, turning a bit red and said, "You got me good, Ben. You really had me going there." Fred gently put the big fish into the live well and then looking at Ben out of the corner of his eyes he said with a joking drawl, "Ya'll better watch yerself' ya'll be gittin yers too, one day soon, ya'll see!"

Ben laughed and after Fred snapped a picture of him holding his big fish, they turned it loose. As Ben watched its form disappear into the dark watery depths he was momentarily overcome with a feeling of wistfulness and again he subconsciously heard Sammi's innocent, gentle, voice, this time as a whisper. It said, "Fwed'll' be okay PamPaw! It's alwight." For a split second, he remembered the fish's eye and the words from before and then he heard a splash. Looking up from the rippling water from whence the fish had disappeared, Ben became shockingly aware that Fred was gone. His mind screamed at him, "The splash? He must have fell in!" Ben stood up in the boat, balancing himself and looking into the water, seeing nothing but deep, dark, and cold mystery. "Fred!... Where are you?... Fred," he hollered. A great fear and foreboding sense of utter dread washed through Ben's mind as he frantically searched over the sides of the boat looking for Fred. After a full minute, Ben was more scared than he had ever been before. His inner reasoning screamed at him, "Fred's got to be stuck down there! You've got to save him!" Ben tore off his fishing vest and stared hard into the water trying to see Fred. He could only see water and pond scum, but his mind kept screaming, "Do something!... Jump in!... Save Fred!... Ben, you stupid idiot, what are you waiting for? Do something!" Ben took a deep breath and plunged over the side of the boat. He expected to feel the shock of the cold water, but instead he only felt himself falling into an endless darkness. He heard a voice screaming, "Fred!... Fred," and realized it was his own. As he continued to fall, panic and fear flooded his very soul until he heard Fred's deep voice, somewhere far away say, "Ben, ya'll kin' let me go, it's okay. Ah'll be jest fine." The voice faded and Ben yelled, "Help me Lord! Someone, please help me! Oh, Fred!" It was cold and dark as Ben continued to fall. He screamed, "Frrrre-e-e-e-e-ed," as he fell, and he fell,... and... fell.

Ben awoke with a start, his heart beating fast, a cold sweat spread across his brow and he hoarsly whispered, "Fred!" It was still dark outside, but he could hear robins and other song-birds beginning to tune up their vocals for another day. Sarah lay softly snoring beside him and Ben realized everything he had just experienced, had been a dream. He breathed a sigh of relief and lay in bed for a few minutes, wondering what the dream could have meant, and why he felt so sad. He never considered the idea that the dream was in prelude, to the actual nightmare, that would become, today. As most dreams do, it's events rapidly faded from Ben's memory, or at least for the time being. Besides, the weatherman had predicted a beautiful day full of sunshine for today, not too hot or cool, but just right. Soon, he started feeling really good. Excitement began to build up in Ben's thoughts as he remembered what day it was, the 29th of September 2006. Today was officially Fred's first full day of retirement from the plant and he and Ben were going to celebrate by going fishing bright and early at the old reservoir South of town.

About a year ago, Ben retired from the same plant after putting in thirty-seven years. He started working there in 1968, just after a twenty-six month stint with the U.S. Army, spending the biggest part of the last fourteen in Vietnam. He and Sarah had been married for five years, with the last two being understandably faith-trying to say the least. Fortunately, God had brought Ben safely home from the war and before too long, Sarah was pregnant with whom would be the couple's only child, a girl they would name, "Amy" after Sarah's grandmother. Being freshly back in the states with a baby on the way, Ben needed to find a job in the worst way. His father got him on at the plant where he worked on the edge of town. It was a factory that made appliances of all sorts, for a world-wide distributor, whose name is yet synonymous today.

At first, it was Ben's idea to stay at the plant only as long as it took to find something better, but it seems he found a niche, and thus, he stuck it out for the long haul. Ben's job in the plant changed every so many years as did the technology in manufacturing. Seemingly much sooner than he ever believed possible, he had twenty years invested into the plant and had moved up the ranks into a position of management. By the twenty-fifth year he had advanced as far as he ever would, but Ben was content with his position there. Despite the constant rumors spread throughout all the years that the plant would close down some day or relocate, Ben had seldom worried, and it's still going strong today. When he was working there, just like most people do in their various occupations, there were days he liked it and days he absolutely hated it. It was no-one's idea of a glamour job, and he surely hadn't gotten rich at it, but he and Sarah were thankful for it. The job had paid the bills, provided insurance, allowed them a yearly vacation and a lifestyle they have been well satisfied with. Now that he was retired, it also afforded him the blessing of living on a pretty awesome pension.

Today, it was Fred's turn to start enjoying the retired side of life, although there were times that Ben thought of it more a just the "Tired side of life." It was going to get better now though, for now he would have someone to do the things with him which he thoroughly enjoyed, but Sarah held no interest in, like fishing.

The farewell party for Fred F. Stone at the plant had been great. Everyone there liked Fred and although most of them hated to see him go, they were also happy for him. After all, he had paid his dues, almost thirty-four years worth. Many of the guys through the years had teased him by calling him "Yabba Dabba Stone," or asking him what it was like to work on the back of a dinosaur, but Fred always knew they meant no harm. He took it all in stride and could even dish it out himself on some occasions. Ben would never forget the time that Fred laced Pete McCall's cigarettes with stink loads the day after Pete had used a marker to draw a cartoon character on Fred's lunch box. Pete had lit up his loaded cancer stick in the break room, surrounded by Ben, Fred and about two dozen of their co-workers. Soon thereafter, he started turning green and the whole room vacated rather quickly with nearly everyone gagging. No one would have ever guessed that mild-mannered, deep-voice, gentle Fred could have orchestrated such a dastardly fiasco. Even Ben would have been clueless had he not happened look at Fred and see him wink as they both exited the break room with their shirts pulled up over their noses. Poor old Pete had to endure the knick-name of, "Stinky," for quite some time after that.

Ben got Fred the job at the plant, just after that special Christmas Eve back in 1972 when they first me. Who would have ever guessed that a dirty unknown stranger could come into a small-town church and so quickly realize that God had steered him from the very brink of utter spiritual desolation and back into the land of the living. Not only did he get a chance at a new life and to make new friends, but he even discovered something he had never thought he would, romance. Just a mere five weeks later, to nearly everyone's surprise, except maybe for Ben and Sarah's, Fred Stone and Martha Whitmoore were married. Their courtship may have been short, but no one who ever knew them, doubted for a instance, that they were destined to be united in "Holy Matrimony" by God himself. A better union was never conceived and as they say, "The rest is history."

Fred, over the course of his years at the plant, didn't advance as far as Ben did, but he never complained, or at least not in a serious manner. Although they worked in different sections of the plant, they always drove and ate lunch together. Their families attended company functions together and each of them respectably had organized one another's retirement parties. Over the last few years, Ben and Fred had been talking about and eagerly looking forward, more and more, to retirement. They promised themselves a special day of fishing, the very first full day, that they were both officially retired. Today, was that glorious day. Just a month ago they traded in Ben's old john-boat and split the cost on a brand new one with a trolling motor, padded seats, a live-well and a trailer. They bought new spin-cast reels and even updated their tackle boxes. Little Sammi had heard them talk so much about this day, that she wanted to join them too, and Ben would have gladly brought her along, but Amy had other plans for her little look-alike that day.

Half an hour after waking, with the eastern sky showing promise that the weatherman had predicted correctly for once, Ben and Fred were both standing on the driveway, where Ben's truck was parked, already hooked up to the new boat's trailer. They had gotten it ready the night before and now they stood silently looking at the boat. It was packed with a cooler, rods, reels and enough fishing equipment to equip a pro-bass fishing tournament. Both men were grinning like school boys preparing to play hookey.

Ben took a deep breath, full of admiration for what he was considering to be, one of the better things in life and turning to his fishing compadre he asked in an exhilarated voice, "Well are you ready to go catch the big-ones, Mr. Officially, Retired, Fred F. Stone?" After emitting a wolf-whistle that seemed too loud to have possibly come from someone of Fred's stature, his even bigger voice resonated off of the side of the house as he answered, "Ready, I am, my good sir! Ben, it's kind of hard to believe. I thought this day would never come. God is sure bein' mighty good to us!" Ben smiled and added, "Yes, he surely is!" Fred turned on his drawl as he went on to say, "Sun's a comin' up an it'd be a fine day ta' meet da Lord! Ya' betta' look out fish cuz' here we come!" Ben was glad, but oddly bothered at the same time, wondering what Fred had meant by, "A fine day to meet the Lord." For a second the dream he'd had just over an hour earlier, tugged at his subconscious. But, then excitement kicked back in quickly and any disconcerting thoughts he may have had were completely forgotten when Fred said with enthusiasm, "Wal' Ben, da' fish be a waitin' fer us! Let's you n' me git' to it!" Ben smiled and replied, "I'm with you Buddy!"

As he sat in his recliner, Ben couldn't help but smile for a bit, as he relived that day, for it had started out great, aside from that confounded dream. The scenes playing out in his mind were so vivid and real that they were much more than just memories. They were all the sane realities which had played part in a seemingly insane totality. Ben's smile faded and was replaced by deep lines of sorrow which etched themselves across his face and forehead. He absolutely hated, what he knew was coming and part of him wanted to get up quickly and go get to work on the snow which had fallen outside over night. He tried to tell his legs to move, but they would not. He felt like screaming for help, but he couldn't. Tears formed in the corners of his eyes again and he was helpless to resist the pull of the 29th of September.

Ben found himself back in the seat of his truck with Fred smiling and chattering aimlessly beside him. In his mind, he kept repeating, "I don't want to be here!... I don't want to be here!" Then a small voice in the back of his head whispered, "Don't worry. It's going to be okay." The voice faded and Ben was behind the steering wheel, listening to Fred and once again, he was eagerly looking forward to a retirement-fishing-celebration. He could even feel the movement of his truck as he and Fred pulled out of his driveway, and he saw the sun, just beginning to peek over the horizon.

Ben turned the radio on low. It was playing a country song about, of all things, fishing. It seems the singer was boldly willing to risk the repercussions of a disgruntled spouse who didn't want him to go fishing. Ben was sure glad that Sarah wasn't like that. Outside the windshield, the world was slowly coming to life and everything felt just right. As the two friends drove down the main drag in town they started bragging about the size of fish they were going to catch that day and what bait was the best to use. After a friendly little debate about who would get the biggest and most fish, they grew quiet to listen to the weather forecast on the radio. As the meteorologist concluded a favorable report Fred pointed up ahead and to the left side of the truck saying, "Thar's Billy a workin' hard at it!" Ben looked over, bumped his horn and waved, to the skinny dark-headed boy of about thirteen, who delivered his newspaper. Fred quickly rolled down his window and hollered, "Yer doin' a good job, Billy!" Billy looked up from his bike, while grabbing a paper out of the bag hanging on the handlebars with a puzzled look at first. Then recognition kicked in and he smiled, waved and hollered, "Hey Mr. Stone... Mr. Chambers!... Catch one fer' me!" As they passed him and his greeting faded away, Fred turned to Ben and said, "He's a good boy, thet' one there."

They passed several tractors and trucks, already hauling loads of grain to the elevator, evidence that the farmer's morning, had started even earlier than Ben and Fred's. "Phewwweeee!... Thet' smells plumb arful," Fred stated as they passed a sanitation truck and it's odiferous contents announced themselves into the sweet morning air. For a moment, Ben just got an evil-eyed stare when he suggested that maybe the smell had come from

Fred and that perhaps he hadn't showered in a while, but then Fred turned the tables when he smiled and countered, "Wal' Ben, Ah' wernt' gonna say a thing, so ah' blamed it on da' truck, but ah' figger'd it was yo' breath." Both men broke out laughing as Ben rolled to a halt behind a school bus with the sign out and kids getting on board. A few youngsters were looking over the back seat at them, but when Fred and Ben waved at them, the kids just stuck their tounges out at them. "Why those little…," Ben started to mutter until he turned to his right and saw Fred returning the gesture with his thumbs in his ears and adding moose antlers to the greeting. "Why you child, your as bad as they are!" Ben exclaimed. Fred just turned to Ben giving him the same greeting and then he replied, "Aw Ben, yer' jest bein' a cranky ole' stick in the mud." Unable to resist the sudden urge to fling out a comeback, Ben said, "I'm a crank, am I?" and then he pointed at Fred and then put his finger and thumb to his forhead in the shape of an "L" like he'd seen some kids on television do. Fred just leaned towards Ben with his eyes rolled upward and asked with a cultured tone, "Who's being the child now?" Both men broke out laughing as the traffic resumed.

A minute later Ben saw Fred pick up and shake his empty thermos and he knew just what his friend was thinking, "Wakey Juice." Martha and Sarah often teased their husbands about being coffee shop connoisseurs. Living up to that reputation was their sworn duty so obviously, they had one stop to make before going to the resevoir. Soon, they were pulling into their favorite café, an old ship-lap sided building with a sign over the door that read, "Just Like Ma's." Anticipation of the savory and deep aroma of java and its rich, dark taste with just a touch of crème made them both hasten a little quicker than usual, towards the front door of the café, but that day, it simply wasn't meant to be.

As Ben sat, sadly remising, he felt a bit guilty, like he should have seen something bad coming. Looking back now in retrospect, he could almost see some sort of pattern emerging from that tragic days events. When he and Fred entered the little café, they had high hopes of satisfying their thirsty palates, but instead they were greeted with the scratchy voice of Sadie Croft, the coffee joint's owner, saying, "Sorry boys! Coffee makers on the fritz today!" Disappoint was only momentary however, because as they headed back out to the truck, Fred suggested, "Let's jest head up da' road, to thet place ne'r the grain elevator. Ya' know thet one thet brags about all dem' drink mixin's." Ben responded, "Okay, let's go." but as they pulled away he thought, "It's just not the same as "Ma's," coffee."

As Ben sat in his living room recliner remembering that thought and it replayed over and over through his mind, he bitterly, but softly said aloud, "It'll never be the same again, old Buddy!" Then his body stiffened and he clutched at the armrests of his chair as his mind returned to that day. They were driving towards the convenience store and talking about weird drink combinations. It was only three blocks from "Just Like Ma's," to the convenience store, but it took a while because they had to stop behind, carefully pass, and wait for several farm vehicles. Tractors and big trucks were everywhere, traveling to and returning from the elevator, driven by farmers, farmers spouses, farmer's kids and their hired hands. Even though farming is different than it used to be, and it's harder than ever for the small family farms to survive, it still stands as one of the key economic backbones of many communities and Ben and Fred's small town just happened to be one of them. Every truck and tractor around Ben's truck today was driven by an honest, hard-working and God-fearing purveyor of the land who entertained high hopes of a bountiful harvest. Each of them viewed their loads as more than just grain, it wasn't simply corn or beans, rather it was their own form of gold from the fields. On the corner of one block, Fred and Ben noticed some young entrepreneurs set up with a lemonade stand, eagerly hoping to make their own meager profits from the thirsty farm crowd driving into town. In farm towns, things like that are a way of life.

Ben had lived in farm country most of his life, and normally he was accustomed to harvest time, but today, he couldn't shake a feeling of nervousness. It was in the form of a dull ache or knot, right in the pit of his stomach and he dismissed it as hunger pains. He figured he'd take care of that at the store when they got to it. Fred was now talking about tractors, farming, ethanol, and the rising price of fuel. That has been one of Ben's pet peeves for a long time, so soon he was on his soap-box, giving Fred his own opinions of how he felt about the big oil companies getting rich at the expence of the American public and what he thought the solution was.

By the time, he and Fred parked in front of the convenience store, they had resolved most of the worlds economic problems and resumed talking about fishing. As they got out of the truck their conversation was forced to cease because the noise of grain trucks, tractors, machinery and people yelling. It nearly impossible to hear anything, seeing as how the elevator was just across the road. Once inside the store, it was quieter and they made their way to the coffee center. As advertised, there were endless choices for creative beverage concoctions, many more than Ben preferred.

After determining which spout dispenced just plain black coffee they filled their thermos's. Ben grabbed a big plastic bottle of powdered creamer which had coffee stains all over it and spooned just the right amount into his thermos. He put the lid on, shook, it up and handed the creamer to Fred. Then he remembered that he was hungry and said, "I'm going to grab a few donuts Fred. Do you want any?" Fred looked up from his thermos and replied, "Naw! Ah' gotta' watch muh girlish figger' ya know." Ben laughed and poked him in the ribs saying, "Why you're so skinny now that you will probably fall over the next time one of us blows out birthday candles. Are you sure you don't want a donut or two, or maybe a dozen?" Fred just smiled and replied, "Naw! B'side's Martha done put sum' cookies in muh' lunch box, an' they's a soundin' pert ne'r good, bout' now."

Ben went and found a few of his favorite donuts, chocolate-iced, pudding-filled long johns. There were two lines at the checkout counter when he got to it. Fred was already in one, standing behind a young woman with two screaming kids, and she sure had her hands full. Fred just grinned and winked at Ben as he got in the other line and somehow he made it to the register before Fred. The young man at Ben's register looked as though he were nursing a hangover and the two screaming kids from the other line were obviously not helping his headache. He rung up Ben's purchases and the total came to two dollars and sixty-two cents. Ben paid with a crumpled five dollar bill from his front pocket, receiving two dollars and thirty -eight cents in change. As the sullen looking clerk handed him the receipt, Ben noticed that he had only been charged for one donut, so he said, "Excuse me, Sir, but you only charged me for one donut and I have two." The clerk quickly developed a look that silently said, "Stupid! Why didn't you tell me that you had two donuts the first time!" as he rung up the second donut and then he said in a dull monotone voice, "That'll be seventy-eight cents, please." As Ben handed over a dollar bill, the clerk managed to mumble thanks, before his voice was lost in the sudden blasting scream of one of the irate children who had been in Fred's line. The poor mother was desperately trying to make her way towards the door with one kid kicking and screaming in her left arm, while trying to carry the bag of her purchases, and drag the other child who was being rather willfully disobedient along, at the same time. Ben looked over at the young mother, feeling her pain, when he heard Fred exclaim, "Aw' shoot! Hey Ben, kin ya' hep' a friend?"

Turning in Freds direction, Ben saw him looking embarrassed as he asked in a more serious, deep voice, "Hev' ya' got two bucks? I done left muh' wallet in the truck." Ben became aware of his own clerk coughing rudely to get his attention and when he turned towards the unpleasant young man he had twenty-two cents thrust into his hand with a dry, "Your change Mister." Ben felt the strong urge to teach the clerk a thing or two about knuckle-sandwiches and professional courtesy, but he resisted the temptation as he heard Fred say, "Ben? Actually ah' jest' need a buck eighty-fo'. Kin ya' hep' me out?" Ben slid over next to Fred and pulled the change out of his pocket. He counted it along with what was in his palm and he only had a total of a dollar sixty. He too, had left his wallet in the truck and had only brought in a five dollar bill. The clerk at Fred's register whom was dressed in Gothic style, had her nose pierced twice and was smacking gum, put her hands on her hips impatiently, exhaled loudly and rolled her stern looking, black mascara lined eyes.

As Ben remembered this moment from his recliner, he cursed himself, for probably the hundredth time since that day. His heartbeat quickened and internally, he screamed at himself. "Why'd you leave your wallet in the truck?... You lousy pig!... Why did you have to have that second donut?... You shouldn't have been honest with that stupid, rude clerk!... Where did your honesty get you?... Blast you Ben Chambers, you only needed twenty four stinking cents!... You would have had enough change for Fred, if you'd kept your mouth shut!... It's your fault! God, you were supposed to look out for him!" Waves of despair washed over Ben as he clutched his chair even harder, and the unfair, cold, and bitter realities of that awful day resumed in his mind.

Ben was standing next to Fred, right there by the register in that convenience store. Fred smiled weakly, muttering, "Ah reckin' ah'd fergit muh head if'n it weren't attached." Then, looking at the scowling female clerk he lost his drawl and said, "If you will excuse me, but for a moment Ma'am, I'll shall return shortly with sufficient payment for my purchase." She just looked at Fred with a sneering look that seemed to sarcastically say, "Whatever!" and then redirected her glare to the next unfortunate customer in line. Ben looked at Fred, giving him a wry smile and a helpless shrug of his shoulder's. He held his hands turned upward and out, as he said, "Sorry Fred." Fred in turn just grinned at Ben and replied, "Tain't nuthin' but a thang, Ben. Ah' reckin' it's all pawt' of da' journey of life."

Ben didn't know why, but he froze for a split second and the hair rose on the back of his neck. Not even he, himself, noticed the chilling pause at the time, for it passed quicker than the blink of an eye. But, it was long enough for the words, "journey of life" to flash through his mind, and imprint themselves as a troubling question which would later assist in haunting his memories. Fred grabbed his thermos and started walking towards the door to go get his wallet so he could pay the clerk dressed in black. For all appearances, she had already forgotten about Fred, for she was loud-smacking her gum and rolling her eyes impatiently at the next customer in line.

Ben started for the door also when, as fate would have it, wouldn't you know, "Murphy's Law," took effect. He accidentally knocked over a box of individual drink mixes that had been laying on the counter and over half of them ended up scattered across the floor. Now, feeling embarrassed himself, especially after getting a sneer from the darkly shadowed eyes of the clerk, Ben knelt down to gather the packets to put them back into the box. Looking towards the front door, Ben saw Fred smiling and holding the door for a familiar looking young woman. The odor of exhaust fumes and the sounds of the traffic outside drifted in. The woman was the same one who had been in line ahead of Fred, with the upset kids. Only one of the kids appeared to be fussing now, and their mother was smiling and saying something, probably thanking Fred for holding the door. "That's my Pal, always the gentleman." Ben thought to himself feeling proud of his friend as he carefully finished gathering the last few drink packets and put them back into the box. He reached for the edge of the counter and started to pull himself up thinking, "These old knee's just don't work like they used to."

Suddenly, the dreadfully sinister howl of tires squealing to stop, drowned out every other noise in and around the convenience store. Ben, bolted to his feet as a cold wave of shear terror tore through his body and his stomach convulsed. In the midst of the horrendous shrieking of the tires, everyone there, heard a sickening thud, followed by the sound of a woman screaming and the deafening impact of a massive crash.

A deafening silence fell over the customers in the store, and Ben was momentarily frozen in place. He stood stunned, looking towards the door, not even seeing the frantic crowd of people already gathering out by the road. Ben remembered his dream, about diving out of the boat and into the darkness while screaming the name which now formed silently at his lips, "Fred." Ben felt his heart skip a beat and his trance was broken when a hysterical man burst through the store's front door, yelling for help. Fear, like he had never experienced before, not even in while in Vietnam, flooded over Ben, as he heard the man's tragic exclamations.

"Someone, Call 911!... Oh my Lord!... That boy,... he fell off the tractor, and that... that... Brave man!... That car, it came from nowhere, and... and... it was moving so fast!... And..." Ben began to feel numb all over, dreading what he knew to be true, yet hoping beyond all measure, that he was mistaken. He earnestly tried to will himself not to hear what the distraught man was going to say next, but to no avail. He started running for the door, praying, "Lord, please, please, I beg of you, don't let it be!" as the man's continuing words echoed in his ears as he tore into the parking lot. "That man!... That poor man! He... he... he came from out of nowhere, and the... the. He saved the boy! Oh my God, someone please call 911!"

Somebody was shouting and a few women were crying, but everything appeared strangely muted to Ben as he rushed past his truck and boat towards the crowd of nervous onlookers, gathered near the road directly across from the grain elevator's entrance. He hurried around the edge of the crowd, scared of what he somehow inwardly knew he would discover, yet refused to believe. There was a tractor attached to a wagon full of corn parked at an odd angle to the left side of the road. A few feet from it, on the graveled shoulder, sat a thin, dark-haired boy of about thirteen with his head in his hands and several adults around him. He appeared to be shaken up, but otherwise, okay. Laying on its side in the gravel at the side of the road, just inches to the right of the boy, lay a dented and familiar looking thermos.

About one hundred feet further up and on the right side of the road was a late model compact car buried underneath the bed of a massive grain truck all the way up to the windshield.

Golden corn was spilling out of a freshly torn hole in the trucks rear tail panel and was mounding up on the crumpled remains of the car. The driver, a balding overweight man with blood running down his face was being helped out of the wreckage by several other people.

The sun was now shining brightly and a row of pigeons sat silently on the roof of the elevator's weigh-in shed, watching the commotion in front of and below them. The smell of burnt rubber wafted on the air and traffic was backing up on each side of the accident. In the distance, the sound of sirens could be heard, and closer to the scene, a tractor, much in need of a new muffler was idling making it hard to hear for the people who were now talking excitedly on their cell-phones. Ben noticed none of these things however, and it was as if he were walking down a long, cold and lonely tunnel. His steps slowed down as his eyes focused on a small group of people standing around a bundle of clothes on the road, half way between the fallen boy and the wrecked car. Ben pushed his way through the people and fell on his knees beside the bundle of clothes crying, "Oh my God! No!" He felt as though a hot knife had just been plunged through his heart, for it was no bundle of clothes,… it was Fred.

Even for Ben, it was hard to recognize the bloody, twisted form that lay on the ground before him. Fred was laying on his back, facing the sky and his torso was convulsing. His head was a gruesome mess, all torn and bloody, while his lower body, from just below the chest was twisted around the other way. One arm was folded underneath him and the other was visibly broken in several places, as were both of his legs and one shoe was missing His chest was moving up and down under his blood soaked shirt, but his breathing was heavily labored and frothy blood was foaming on his busted lips. His nose was broken, his eyes closed and every other second his head would twitch, each time, making Ben cringe violently.

Even though deep inside Ben would later have to admit to himself that he knew that Fred wasn't going to make it, he willed himself to believe that he was going to survive the accident, anyway. He convinced himself that God would keep Fred alive, heal him and everything would be okay. He heard someone say the ambulance was on its way, and he wished it were already here. He wasn't going to say "Good bye," to his friend,... not this way,... not today. They were supposed to go fishing and celebrate retirement! With tears in his eyes, he leaned over Fred's still form and said, "Hang in there Buddy, you're going to make it," and then he silently prayed with his tears flooding down his cheeks and his whole body shaking, "Dear heavenly Father. Please, oh please God, bless Fred to be okay. You and you alone can save him, I know you can and I believe that you will! Please God, in Jesus name I pr....!"

Ben's prayer was cut short and a glorious wave of momentary joy washed over him when Fred suddenly groaned and opened his eyes. They were clear as a bell and looking around until they locked on to his own eyes. Ben had to clear his throat as he wiped the tears from his own eyes and uttered, "Thank you God!... You're going to be fine Fred! You're going to make it!" Fred coughed and blood sprayed from his smashed nose and lips. Ben could see that even his teeth and left cheek bone were shattered. He became aware that Fred was trying to say something, but he couldn't make out his words. Leaning in close, almost touching Fred's bloody lips with his ear, Ben could finally hear the question, "Did I save the boy?" Ben turned, looking Fred in the eyes and answered, "You sure did Buddy! You were a hero today!" Fred's normally deep voice was only a hoarse, soft, whisper now as he slowly nodded his head and said, "Good." His head twitched again as he stared at Ben and after coughing up more blood, he whispered, "That one Christmas,... Thanks fer takin' me in." Then his body jerked violently and he gasped for breath, closed his eyes and uttered, "Ya been a good friend ta' me, Ben Chambers." Tears welled up in Ben's eyes once more and fears' icy grasp seized his heart as internally he screamed, "No!... Help him God!" He was panicking on the inside, but outwardly he kept looking into Fred's eyes saying, "You're going to be okay Fred, just hang in there.... the ambulance is almost here! Don't give up!... Stay with me Fred!... We've got fish to catch and your retirement to celebrate!... Come on Buddy, you can do it!"

Ben looked up at the bystanders gathered around feeling completely helpless as he screamed, "Where's that ambulance?" One of the men standing there craned his neck, looking over the crowd, pointed and said, "There it is! It's coming from right over there!" The siren was louder and soon everyone could hear the racing motor of the ambulance, that is, everyone except for Ben and Fred. Fred had opened his eyes again and between bloody coughs and body twitches he whispered to Ben. "She was right Ben, it's gonna be okay." Ben fought back tears as he asked, "Who was right, Fred?" Fred's voice was getting weaker and he whispered slower and softer, as he went on, "My Ma was right. Look at that Ben." Fred motioned upwards with his eyes. Ben glanced up frantically seeing nothing, but the bright sunlight and asked, "At what Fred? What is it?" Ben had to lean in close again to make out his friends voice. At first, all he could hear was wheezing and a bubbling noise coming from deep inside Fred's lungs, but then he made out his words. "Ben, ah' told ya it were a good day ta' meet the Lord." Ben leaned back, looking intensly into Fred's eyes and yelled, "No Fred!... You've got to hang on! It's not your time!... Not today!... Not like this! It's not fair!" Fred coughed up more blood and rasped, "It's fixin' ta' be alright, Partner!... It's all jest' a pawt' of the journey."

Ben looked up hysterically and saw the ambulance with it's doors open and the E.M.T.'s rushing towards he and Fred. He looked back down at Fred saying, "See! They're here! You're going to be okay and...!" Ben stopped talking as his eyes suddenly fixated on Fred and everything seemed to be moving in slow motion. Somehow, Fred had raised his bloodied head up and was looking right at Ben's face. It was as if he were staring right into Ben's soul and trying to say something. Ben grasped Fred's hand, forgetting about the broken arm and he stared hard into his best friends eyes and pleaded, "What is it Fred?" At first, the words wouldn't come, but when they did, Ben felt something vital inside of himself, break. Fred whispered, "Ah' know'd muh' time were comin' soon.... ah' reckon ah's ready.... Ben, you make sho' thet' yer okay with Him." (Fred's eyes motioned upward for an instant.)

He coughed again and lay his head back down on the blood-soaked ground, with his eyes still locked on Ben's, gasping, "Ben?" Ben's lips quivered and his tears fell even harder as he felt like his heart was being ripped from his chest and he asked, "What is it Fred?" As he lay there on the hard, cold ground, with his life rapidly seeping from his body, Fred's eyes turned sad for just a moment and a single tear streaked down his bloodied cheek as he softly whispered, "Ben, you tell Martha,... I'll see her later. (he coughed again)... Tell her that she's the best part of muh' life an' (he coughs violently several more times)....and th... tha...that I love her!" Ben began sobbing like a baby and convulsions tore through his body as he promised, "I will Fred! I will!" Fred's eyes rolled up ward and the sadness Ben saw there just seconds ago suddenly disappeared and they looked curious. The curiosity faded and suddenly, even with his broken lips and teeth, Fred smiled and a great sense of excitement seemed to come into his eyes and he appeared to be at peace. Ben was so moved by this transformation that he stopped sobbing and just stared. As the E.M.T.'s rushed up, Fred, turned to Ben and deliberately winked at him and then with his voice low and slow, but deep and baritone like it had always been before and a renewed excitement glowing from his eyes he said, "It's Him!... He's here, Ben!... I made it!" Fred laid back, smiled even bigger and his face seemed to glow, like it had that one Christmas Eve thirty-four years ago,... and he died.

Ben sagged down in his recliner feeling numb all over, not moving or even aware of anything except a great weight of sadness that seemed to be bearing down on him. Fred was gone and poor Martha had been devastated. His dear friend was laid to rest during a small ceremony at the church and Ben remembered being moved by the huge number of people who showed up to pay tribute to such a great man. He hadn't been rich or hugely successful by modern day society's standards, but he had most definitely left a lasting positive impression on everyone he ever met.

The newspaper article told about the accident and the amazing hero Fred had been. How, with not a single thought as to his own safety, he came darting out from nowhere, and safely shoved aside the young boy whom had fallen from the tractor, and was himself in turn, struck by the speeding car of a man who had been in a hurry, running late for work and talking on his cell phone. It said that he left behind a widow, the former Martha Whitmoore and that they had no children. The paper also reported that Fred was a Vietnam veteran and a decorated war hero. Ben hadn't known about Fred's medals for he had never mentioned them. Neither did Ben know that Fred's parents had died together in a tragic fire many years ago. Fred never talked much about his past to anyone, not even Ben, but you know the newspapers. They have a way of digging things up. The obituary told about Fred's retirement from the plant and of his community and church involvements. It ended with the posting of the wake and funeral times, followed by a suggestion as to where memorials could be sent and that was it. As far as a stranger could tell, Fred's life was encompassed in a black and white photograph of his smiling face followed by two small paragraphs.

Fred had been well liked and would be greatly missed by those who knew him best, but as for those who did not know him, perhaps a few would read the article, and at least for a minute or two, and think about the hero he was. Sadly, it would probably be only a momentary pause in their own lives, before they continued on living and quickly forgetting his name. "I'll never forget you Buddy!" Ben whimpered.

Suddenly breaking through the misty fog of his morose thoughts, Sarah's voice startled him into alertness. "Ben, are you alright?" she asked with great concern. Ben sat up looking at his watch, surprised that it was already 7:30 a.m. and remembered the snow outside. He looked at Sarah immediately composing himself, smiled and said, "Good morning Dear! I'm was just thinking about, well, You know,... Fred!" Sarah came over and put her hand on his shoulder asking, "Are you okay, Dear?" She knew the truth because she could see the tear stains on his cheeks. Ben tried his best to hide his pain from everyone, but his beautiful bride could always see through his façade. Ben stood up, turned to Sarah and hugged her tightly, loving her even more at the moment than he had when they first got married. It's funny, but she always thought of Ben as being her rock, but secretly, Ben got his strength from her love. Without her by his side, he feels like he is nothing.

Sometimes, and especially since the accident, her hugs were the only things helping him to maintain any sense of sanity. Even though he wishes that he could say that it is his faith in the Lord, that keeps him facing each day with what many perceived to be strength and integrity, Ben knows that it really is the love he and Sarah share. He realizes the credit should go to God, and he even feels guilty that he can't seem to force himself to feel that way he knows he is supposed to, but he had a secret buried so deep inside of his heart, that he hadn't even dared to admit it to himself, yet. Way down within the innermost realms of Ben's tormented soul, lies a secret so obscure that only the Creator knows. Ben cannot voice such an atrocity aloud. He has been taught never to think it, consider it and God forbid, possibly ever feel it, but the sad truth is that Ben is furious at God. He secretly blames God for taking Fred away, and even though he can lie to himself, to Sarah, and to everyone who cares about him by saying, "I'm okay" he really,... is not. Will he ever let himself be right inside again? Perhaps not. But then again, Hey! Christmas is more than just a holiday, it's the time of miracles, right? For those so bold as to simply believe,... we'll see.

CHAPTER EIGHT

The sound of a snowplow grating on the road outside as it pushes last nights snow echoes throughout the house. After quickly washing down his last bite of scrambled eggs with some orange juice and looking at Sarah he grins, saying, "I'd better get to it. It sounds like the competition is out ahead of me." Smiling back at Ben, Sarah teases him saying, "Competition, swampitition. You know that you just want to get out and play in the snow." Ben got up and made his way around the table to Sarah and kissed her on the neck until she squirmed. He asked her if she wanted to come along, but already knew the answer to that absurd question. It was Christmas Eve and there was a ton of things needing done yet.

Ben was going to plow snow most of the morning while Sarah planned to do the breakfast dishes, throw together a crock pot full of delicious home-made chili for supper and then go into town to tie up some last-minute Christmas things. She had promised Amy that she and Martha would come over by 11:00 a.m. to help bake cookies, wrap Christmas presents for Sammi, and then hide them away, so Santa could make his miraculous deliveries later tonight. Joe, Sammi's father, had to work until 3:30 p.m. so to Ben's delight, it was his duty to pick up and hang out with Sammi until her mother and grandmother finished their secret advent mission. At 4:30 p.m. Ben was supposed to take Sammi back home and pick up Martha and take her home.

Hopefully, sometime before church started, he and Sarah would have a chance to determine how the pot of chili had turned out.

They had last-minute presents of their own to wrap, and many to take out of hiding and place around the tree. They also had some appetizers to fix for the family to enjoy later in the evening and somehow in the midst of all the hustle and bustle, find time to get themselves cleaned up and dressed. Then, they needed to pick up Sarah's mother, Helen at the assisted living villa in town, swing back towards home and pick up Martha next door, and hurry off to the Christmas Eve program at church. It started at 7:15 p.m. but, the plan was to be there by 6:50 p.m. so they could get a seat. As in most every church to be found, Christmas Eve and Easter were the two times a year you had to arrive early to guarantee a seat. After the service they would go home, soon followed by Sammi and her parents to see if Old St. Nick had been there, play games, sing carols and of course, they would pig out like there was no tomorrow.

For several years now, Ben's folks had been coming over to his family's house to enjoy a huge dinner and to celebrate Christmas Day. The big meal used to be held at their house, but John and Theresa Chamber's were well into their nineties now. They could still get around pretty good, but they liked to go to bed early and now days, preparing for large gatherings, was better suited to the younger members of the Chambers family.

Fred and Martha always joined the family as well, but sadly this year, there will be one less smiling face in the crowd, and possibly two, if Ben doesn't find a way to cheer up. In the afternoon, they all will carry out a tradition, Ben started when Amy was a little girl that they like to call, "Jesus Birthday Gift." It had become one of everyone's favorite ways to celebrate the birth of the savior, especially Fred's.

Sometime today or tomorrow morning, Sarah will baked a double-chocolate fudge cake with white icing on it and the words, "Happy Birthday Jesus!" made out of chocolate chips across the top. This year, the whole family and Martha will gather around the dining room table and sing the "Birthday" song as Sarah slowly carries the sweet delicacy into the room with a single candle burning brightly in the center to symbolize the one true way to eternal life. The youngest member of the "Chambers" clan always receives the honor of blowing out the candle and licking the frosting off of it. Once again this year, it will be sweet, adorable Sammi. Then everyone will join together in a verbal prayer thanking Jesus for something that is special to them in their lives. After they each properly dispose of a piece of the cake and a scoop or two of French vanilla bean ice cream, it will be gift time. The gift, is simply where each member of the family will receive an envelope, a pen and a piece of paper on which they will secretly write, a special gift or part of themselves that they wish to give Jesus for his birthday. After everyone finishes writing, they will seal the envelopes and Ben will gather them and put them in a safe place. On Easter when the family gets together to celebrate the glorious resurrection of Jesus Christ, they will open the envelopes and share with everyone, what their gift to Him, had been. It will hopefully be, as it always has been in the past, a time of precious memories, but that's on tomorrow's agenda. Ben and Sarah are currently more concerned with what needs to be done before the church service tonight.

Later today, Ben is supposed to stop by "Lawson's Deli," to pick up a couple of cheese and sausage trays that Sarah ordered for their holiday get-togethers. Then he is supposed to deliver a platter of home-made cookies and candy to Billy, the paperboy. Sarah herself, after helping Amy, wants to personally deliver a few little Christmas baskets she has thrown together and pick up one last surprise for Ben. So as you can see, Ben and Sarah have a typical, run, run, run, try to cram it all in, American Christmas Eve, planned.

Ben was heading for the door when Sarah's voice rang out. "Hey Dear!" He turned to see her looking back over her shoulder at him while standing at the kitchen sink with her arms elbow deep in soapy water as she said, "Please, don't forget to put the cam-corder on the charger, okay? We need to get Sammi's angel performance at the church on disc tonight." Ben was looking forward to seeing Sammi in her angel costume all decked out in a white satiny gown with a gold garland halo perched atop her tiny head and cardboard and cotton wings affixed to her back. He most definitely wanted to record it, so he hurried into the study, sat the camcorder in its dock and after making sure the charger's light turned green, he returned to the back door and put on his coat, gloves, boots, and hat. Then Ben groaned inwardly as he saw that absolutely atrocious looking scarf, Sarah kept insisting that he wear, hanging from one of the coat hooks. "I hate that ugly thing," Ben murmured under his breath. Then he had an idea. "I'll just act like I didn't see it, or better yet I'll hide it under Sarah's coat, so she'll think that she covered it up by mistake, and it'll be her fault I didn't wear it."

Ben smiled, proud as a peacock of his ingenious intuitiveness, however his moment was short lived when Sarah, whom had viewed him over her shoulder and somehow, mysteriously read his mind, suddenly hollered, "Honey, don't forget your scarf." Ben's shoulders sunk with a sigh and his smile slowly wilted into a tell-tale frown of defeat. With a feeling of disdain, he reluctantly reached for the scarf, grabbed it off of the coat hook and looked at it as if it would give him the plague. He hollered at Sarah who was doing the dishes across the room, at the kitchen sink, "I don't know why you think I need this silly scarf. It makes me look like a dork." Sarah dried off her hands, smiled wryly shaking her head and walked across the room giving him another version of, "The look," the one that silently says, "You know, I'm always right." She grabbed the scarf from his hands and started wrapping it around his neck stating, "You'll catch yourself a cold without it. Besides, who wants a cold on Christmas and by the way, you don't look like a dork."

Ben shrugged his shoulders, giving up the battle in what he knew to be a "no win" situation and decided the infernal rag would come off of his neck the minute he got into the shed where his truck was parked. He kissed Sarah saying, "Last chance to frolic in the snow with me" and as he opened the door she returned, "You'll have to play by yourself today,... my hand-some... Dork!"

Ben would have had a snappy response for her, but as the door closed behind him he was momentarily blinded by the brilliant white wonderland his yard had become overnight. As his eyes adjusted to the glare, he looked across the yard, out to the tire swing and all around marveling at the beauty of nature. A pair of squirrels were running up and down the old apple tree and a mixture of cardinals, blue jays and other birds scrambled around in the snow beneath the birdbath which Ben had been using as a feeder lately. The "rat-a-tat," of a woodpecker drumming on the side of a tree somewhere echoed across the yard and Ben thought he saw a red-tailed hawk disappear into the distant clear blue sky. The dripping sound of melting snow came to Ben's ears and he noticed icicles had already started to form, hanging from the house's gutters. Drops of water fell to the ground off of their tips and as a small gust of cold wind blew a swirl of snow off of the awning over the house's kitchen window.

Ben took a deep breath, liking the feeling of the icy air in his lungs and headed for his shed. He had put the blade on the truck three days ago with some doubt in his mind, when the weatherman started predicting a white Christmas, but as the snow scrunched under his boots today, he mused, "Who would have believed it? For once, the guy was right." At least for the moment, Ben forgot the sadness which had plagued him so much since Fred died and he himself, was feeling very much alive.

He opened the side door to the shed, flipped on the light and saw a mouse take off out of the bin where he kept ears of corn for the squirrels. "If he weren't so darn cute, I'd get a cat," Ben thought to himself as he walked over, unhooked the big door and slid it open. Sunlight streamed into the shed as Ben fired up his truck and pulled it out into the eight or so inches of snow on the drive. He turned the heater on full blast, tore his scarf off and threw it into the passenger seat and got out. He marched back into the shed, stomping snow off of his boots and quickly decided what he wanted to do before he left. Next to the corn bin was a metal garbage can full of birdseed with an empty coffee can sitting on top. Ben walked over, tucked three ears of corn under his arm, scooped the can full of seed and headed towards the side door, flipped off the light switch and grabbed a snow shovel with his free hand.

As he plodded through the snow, Ben kicked it up into the air ahead of himself like a kid while he progressively made his way around the yard. Sarah laughed at him, shaking her head from inside of the kitchen window where she had just happened to glance out at him. "There's the Ben I used to know," she thought to herself. After a knock on the window and a wave to her overgrown boy, she got back to her busy schedule.

A few years ago, Fred and Ben had made some squirrel feeders out of cedar two by fours. They were simply made of two pieces, a verticle back, about a foot long and a horizontal piece about six inches long attached to it, to make a shelf. The shelf had a large nail sticking up out of the center of it which skewered the ear of corn. Ben had screwed a feeder to the sides of the big old maple with the tire swing, a white oak by the apple tree and one on a wild cherry tree standing by the bird bath. Ben removed the bare cobs on each of the feeders, and slid a new ear onto each nail. Before he even made it to the second feeder, one hungry squirrel was already atop of the first, barking up a storm as if to say, "What took you so long!"

The birds around the birdbath took off in a frenzied flurry of wings as Ben approached, but they didn't go too far. They perched themselves atop the house and in surrounding tree branches as he brushed the snow off the top of the birdbath and dumped the coffee can's contents into it. By the time he reached the front drive with the snow shovel, the birds were back at the bird bath, happily singing, foraging, and vying for the tastiest morsels.

Across the road, the "Rodgers" boys were busily constructing a snowman. All around town and throughout the countryside, fun would abound today. School was out and the glorious snow which had fallen overnight was the perfect kind for packing. Everywhere, kids of all ages would erect snowmen and forts, engage in snowball fights and go whisking down snow-covered hillsides screeching with glee. The sun felt great in contrast to the winter chill and despite himself, Ben was starting to feel a little tingle of Christmas spirit. He hollered, "Merry Christmas Jim and Tom," and waved to the neighbor boys. "Merry Christmas, Mr. Chambers," the boys returned just before Jim blasted Tom with a snowball. Ben laughed to himself as he thought, "Oh, to be a kid again." He resisted the temptation to reach down for a handful of snow and wing one across the road at the boys. He had been known in the past, to let one fly at Sarah on occasion, but for some reason, she seldom seemed to appreciate it. She simply just didn't respond to a good old snowball splattering like little Sammi did when he'd toss one in her direction. Sammi always just giggled and wanted more.

Ben cleared the sidewalk and porch with the shovel and then using his truck and blade, he removed the snow from the gravel drive leading to the shed and the concrete drive in front of the garage. He was sprucing up the edges near the house with the snow shovel and a broom, humming, "Let it Snow" when the garage door started going up. A few seconds later Sarah came rushing out to give him a kiss, push something into his hands and almost before Ben could return a, "Bye honey. I love you" she was backing the car out of the drive, past his truck and taking off in a hurry towards town.

It was Ben's turn to laugh and shake his head in amusement and looking down at his hands, he was pleased to see that Sarah had given him his thermos. He wondered if it held coffee or cocoa, but as another snowplow went by on the road he remembered that he had to blade off Old Man Shipley, a fellow plant retiree's, driveway. Also, as the church's "Head Trustee," it was up to him to make sure that the parking lot and walks there, were cleared before the Christmas Eve program tonight. He had a lot to get done, so quickly he decided to wait until later to discover the contents of the thermos. Ben felt pretty good having gotten a little exercise in the frosty morning air, but as he remembered that he needed to plow Martha's drive also, his shoulder's sagged a bit and the sorrow of missing Fred assaulted his heart once more. He looked down, feeling depression knocking at the door to his soul once again and he would have given in to the misery had not a jacked up car of teens gone flying by on the road in front of the drive. They had the vehicle's stereo blasting some Christmas rap song so loud, that he could still hear the bass pounding ten seconds later.

Ben looked into the direction of the rapidly disappearing car shaking his head. Then he looked up and said, "It's Christmas Lord and I've got a lot to do. No time for sorrow, now." Lifting his head and willing himself to think good thoughts, he forced himself to smile. The smile became natural rather quickly as he mentally pictured how Sammi would look in her angel costume tonight. He put the shovel and broom into the back of the truck, closed up the garage and shed, ran into the house to grab his cell phone and by the time he got into the truck he had resumed humming Christmas tunes. He switched on the radio just in time to hear the D.J. say, "… you all! Have tons of fun in that snow out there kids and to all of my listeners, sliding around out there, M-e-e-e-e-e-e-e-r-r-r-r-r-r-y Christmas!" A Country Christmas classic started to play as Ben raised the blade, shifted into drive and pulled out into the road and headed to his next stop for the day. Back in his yard, a blue jay was angrily squawking at a squirrel which had just jumped into the birdbath full of seed. The squirrel ignored the irate bird of blue, until he had a mouth full of sunflower seeds and then he was off across the yard and up a tree to enjoy his spoils.

Across the road, Jim and Tom Rodgers were using plastic buckets to scoop snow and build a fort, pausing every so often to pelt one another with snowballs. A jogger ran by on the snow-covered sidewalk near the road and he could smell hickory smoke coming from someone's fireplace. Some people probably think that he's crazy for running in the snow, but he's not concerned with what anyone thinks. He has his headphones on, but his mind is too busy to notice the music. He's a bit worried, not about falling, but about making his wife happy because he has yet to pick out her Christmas present.

A commuter bus suddenly rumbles by him on the road emitting a black cloud of exhaust fumes. When the air finally clears and he stops coughing he realizes there was an advertisement on the side of the bus for a new laptop computer, the same one his wife had been looking at, down at the mall, just the other day. He picks up his pace and hurries towards home, because now he knows what to get her. As his breathing becomes more labored, he thinks of a new worry. Will any of the stores still have one of the computers? What will he do if they don't, for after all, it is Christmas Eve.

CHAPTER NINE

"Mmmm! Mmmmmmm! Mom, these cookies are sho' de'lish," said twelve year old Jacob as he reached over and pushed the back of his eleven year old brother, Eric's head while adding, "Aren't they good, Fart-breath?" Eric reached down grabbing a handful of snow, and threw it in his brother's face warning, "Quit it you,… You,… Pea Brained Idiot!" Jacob flew off of the step where he was sitting and tackled Eric, the momentum causing them to both tumble off of the sidewalk and into a freshly shoveled pile of snow. "Mom, get him off me," Eric screamed. Monica Ames turned red with embarrassment, but the boys had finally managed to light her anger fuse. Before Ben's and her son's eyes, she appeared to grow two feet taller and yelled, "Will you two hoodlums quit it! Why, it's Christmas Eve and you have the nerve to call yourselves, preacher's sons? You both ought to be ashamed of yourselves! Now, stand up, shake hands, apologize to Mr. Chamber's here and for heaven's sake, try to be good. Do you think you can manage that for at least a few minutes?"

Ben fought to keep a straight face as the boy's stood up awkwardly with snow crusted onto their clothing, chocolate chip stains smeared on their faces and looking down like two willfully disobedient puppies. Their mother stood in front of them with her hands on her hips and ordered, "Now, apologize and shake!" The two momentary deviants were so reluctant in their shaking of hands, that it appeared as though they each feared that the other possessed some kind of dangerous disease and their apologies were barely discernable. Then Monica sharply asked them, "Now, what do you say to Mr. Chambers?" They both looked down at their feet and mumbled, "We're sorry Mr. Chambers." Their mother took a step towards them, exhaling loudly and asked with a stern voice, "What did you say? I couldn't hear you, and look at Mr. Chambers, when you speak to him." The boys looked up, Eric rolling his eyes and in a sullen, but defeated voice, they both reluctantly repeated, "Sorry Mr. Chambers."

Ben tried to make his voice sound stern as he looked each boy in the eyes and said, "It's okay boys. I really do appreciate you two young men helping me with the snow. I don't know what I'd of done without your assistance." Then he smiled at the rival siblings who grinned back in return. "Are we done now? Mom, can we go play?" asked Jacob. Monica looked out across the church parking lot which was now clear of snow and at the sidewalks, all of which were clean, except for right up around the steps where she, Ben and the boys were. "You'd better ask Mr. Chambers here, boys," she answered.

Ben knew that the boys were anxious to be off to engage in a snowball fight with their friends down the street. They had talked about it earlier and now, he could see the pleading hopefulness in their eyes as they looked up at him sitting at the top of the church's steps. Ben knew how awesome a good snowball fight could be and he wanted the boys to go enjoy themselves, but just to be ornery a bit, he drug out his answer. Monica stood by silently and smiled. It was doing her heart good to see her boy's figit and squirm as Ben slowly stood up, looked around the area himself, and taking his sweet old time, he said, "Well, you both did a pretty good job of helping to clear the snow,.... . but there's still a bit left,.... . up around these steps. We've got to put these shovels and brooms away. (He pointed to the tools leaned up against the church's doors.) and then,... We need to salt it all down so the people can get safely in and out of the church tonight,... You know. You have really worked hard this morning though, and might I say, it's a fine job you've both done,... and I guess,... well, I reckon I could, maybe finish it by myse...!"

Before Ben could finish the last word the boy's took off like a herd of wild banshee's across the parking lot in front of the church yelling, "Thanks!" while at the same time, pushing each other around as they went. When they were at the end of the building, Monica and Ben could hear the boys calling each other ingeniously, creative, gross names again and then they were gone. Monica turned to Ben with an embarrassed smile and said, "I must apologize for the boys terrible behavior Ben. Sometimes Rick and I don't know what to do with them." Ben just grinned at her and replied, "Monica, don't you worry about it. You and Pastor Rick have some great, rambunctious boys there. They're just being boys, and the name calling, well that's what brothers do." Monica just smiled saying, "I guess your right Ben. You have brother's, and a sister, don't you?" After he nodded she continued, "Did you guys fight too, when you were kids?" Ben inhaled deeply, straightening his back, and with a slight air of aloofness, he turned his head and in a voice showing just a fake hint of being a snob whom had been offended, he answered, "Why, of course not. I have no idea what you could possibly be talking about. We were perfect angels of course!" Then turning back towards Monica with a chuckle, he added, "Just don't ask my parents, okay?" Monica laughed as she started gathering the plates she had brought the cookies out on.

Ben mentally pictured his younger siblings, two brothers, Jack and Steve, and a sister named Julie. In his mind, he had the tendency to picture them more like they had been when they were all kids, because he hadn't seen much of them since he got out of the Army. None of them ever seemed to make it back home very often and they only talked occasionally on the phone. The only time he actually sees them these days, is at weddings, funerals, and once every blue moon.

Jack is sixty-four, retired and living on the East coast where he and his wife Nancy raised their own family. Steve is sixty-two, twice divorced with four kids, a boy and a girl, from each marriage. He seldom saw the kids when they were young and now that they are in their twenties and thirties with lives of their own, he'd like to. He'd just love the chance to get to know them and to try to make up for lost time, but three of the four, want no part of him now. He has a girlfriend young enough to be his daughter and he is a pilot for a major airline. He calls the West coast home, somewhere out in Oregon. Julie is the baby of the family at forty-eight and she became a military wife and traveled the world. She and her husband, Retired Colonel, Edmond R. Walters had no children and they currently reside in France, where he was last stationed.

There is no doubt, that Ben, his brothers, and his sister still love one another, but life has steered them into different directions. In the early years, they all missed each other quite a bit, but absence doesn't always make the heart grow fonder. Now days, they seldom even thought about each other. Ben wished all of them well, but the brother he now missed more than anyone, wasn't blood-kin, but he had been his best friend. Sitting there on the church steps, while Monica finished cleaning up, Ben remembered clearing snow from the church property last year. Fred had helped him that day and Monica had brought out cookies then as well, with her two grappling boys in tow. Fred sure loved those cookies and even more, he liked to tease the boys. "He would have been a great father." Ben thought to himself sadly.

For a moment, sadness rushed back in try and dampen his day and Monica could see it in his eyes. As a pastor's wife, she had seen that look many times before. Even though Ben thought he kept his feeling well hidden from everyone, anybody who really knew him, was aware of how he had felt about Fred and how difficult things have been for Ben ever since that awful accident. Monica could almost read Ben's thoughts now as she glanced into his sad eyes and her heart went out to him. She too, had just adored that wonderful Mr. Stone. She missed his deep voice and friendly smile at church on Sundays, but she could take joy in knowing that even though the accident had been horrible, and that Mr. Stone's loved ones were hurting deeply, that he wasn't in any pain at all. He had bravely saved another family from having to experience a possible tragic loss of their own and now he was in Heaven, where all believers hope to go one day. Monica wished that she knew of a sure way to somehow, give Ben that same comfort she had.

She pictured a plaque in Rick's study, which sat on a little wall mounted shelf beneath a picture of his dearly departed Grandma Ruthie. The picture had been there ever since she and Rick had received the call to this church. His Grandma Ruthie had always loved and been so proud of him. She said that when he became a pastor, it was like an answer to her prayers. Rick loved her dearly, and often still in his sermons, he credits her for his strong faith in the Lord. She fought cancer for nearly two years and she was strong through it all. At a certain point, when she knew her time was near, she could have understandably been weakened in her faith and beg for everyone's pity, but instead, she helped everyone else to stay strong. She comforted her family by saying she was ready to move on, and talking about how great eternity with Jesus would be.

How she got it, no one ever knew, but one day she asked Rick to open the top drawer of the cabinet next to her hospital bed. In it was a small, flat, wrapped and heavy gift with his name written on it. She made him promise that he wouldn't open it until she was gone. Rick promised and took it home with him, and put it on the desk in his church office. Over the next few days, his grandma grew worse and Rick and his entire family became a bundle of nerves. Rick was hard at it, praying by her bedside and with the other family members, but he still had to perform his duties at the church as well. The gift he had placed on his desk got covered up with paperwork and he completely forgot about it. His grandma passed away a few days later, and despite the fact that Rick was a pastor, he was devastated. For a week after the funeral he struggled with his emotions. One day when he was working at his desk, jotting down his thoughts in a little notebook for his sermon for the next Sunday, he just couldn't seem to focus. At one point, he looked up at the picture of his grandma, got to thinking about her and started crying hysterically. Suddenly, for reasons he couldn't explain, he felt anger surge through his body, and untrue to his character, he cursed and violently threw his notebook across the desk.

The notebook scattered a huge pile of papers and sailed across the room hitting the wall just beneath his grandmother's picture. Rick immediately felt ashamed of himself, asking God to forgive him and he looked at the smiling face of his grandma. Her eyes seemed to say, "It's okay Rick. I still love you." Rick got up and collected the notebook and started to gather the disarrayed papers, when suddenly, on the corner of his desk, he saw the wrapped gift from his grandma. With his hands shaking and tears running down his face, he opened it and inside was just what he needed. A gift of love in the form of a small black marble plaque with white letters inscribed across it which read,

"You've always made me so happy,
with all you've said and done.
Don't be bitter, but smile for me,
Cause' now I'm with the Heavenly One!"

After finding that plaque, Pastor Rick tore out of his office to find Monica and he shared with her all that had happened. Those words from his Grandma Ruthie's plaque inspired his sermon that weekend and had given him a renewed vigor in his preaching ever since. Those four simple verses helped Rick to hang onto his faith and motivated him to be truly happy again. Monica wished now, that she had words which could do the same for Ben. Her mind just drew a blank however, so she thought it best not to mention Fred at all.

Ben shook his head, dispelling the foreboding thoughts he was having, put on a smile and said, "Monica, thanks so much for the cookies. You know, I'm sure looking forward to the program tonight. Little Sammi's going to be an angel, you know?" Monica was relieved to hear some cheer in Ben's voice as she responded, "Your quite welcome Ben. Sammi's already an angel, isn't she?" As she turned to head back to the parsonage she added, "Ben thanks for cleaning up around here and we'll see you tonight. Merry Christmas!" Ben grabbed the stair rail and pulled himself to his feet, feeling just a bit stiff from sitting too long and he hollered after her, "Tell Pastor Rick hello for me and Merry Christmas!" The cookies had been delicious, but now Ben needed to wash them down with something and he remembered the thermos Sarah had fixed for him this morning. He hobbled to the truck, working out the kinks he had developed from shoveling snow that morning and he felt good about what he had accomplished thus far.

While opening his truck door and grabbing his thermos, he saw that it was just five minutes after eleven. "I'm making good time today." Ben thought to himself as he unscrewed the thermos and was pleased to find it full of steaming hot cocoa with little white swirls which had to have been the melted remains of little white marshmallows, floating on top. As he slowly drank a cup full of the chocolate ambrosia, he reflected on what he had done so far today and what still remained on his "To Do" list. He gotten his own place shoveled out and the critters fed. Old Man Shiply's place was finished and Martha's drive was done as well. Hers hadn't taken long, just a few swipes of the blade and about ten minutes of shoveling and sweeping, but it had been the most difficult. He had talked to Martha a few minutes and she seemed to be doing okay, but he knew that this holiday season had been torture for her. She seemed to hide her sorrow well though and she was looking forward to going with Sarah to Amy's today.

Ben finished the hot chocolate and got back to shoveling and sweeping. Ten minutes later, the walk was clean in front of the steps and his snow removal duties for the day were done. He went into the church, got the rock salt out of a closet and went back out and sprinkled it up and down the steps and on the sidewalks. He was completely finished and back in his truck at ten till noon.

A modern Christmas classic, with dogs barking out the melody, blared from the radio when Ben fired up his truck. He raised the blade and circled the parking lot to look at the job he had just finished and he was satisfied. Everything looked good and the snow was beginning to melt, but something sticking up out a mound of snow across the pavement caught his eye. It was a wooden handle with lime green neon paint on the end, and he knew instantly that it had to be his own snow shovel. Most likely it was the one young Eric had been playing air guitar on, and shoveling with.

A bunch of sparrows foraging on the edge of the freshly plowed lot, took off as Ben pulled up to the pile of snow. He got out, grabbed the shovel and as he put it in the bed of his truck, a cardinal's sweet melody pierced the air. Suddenly, Ben thought he heard Fred's deep drawl, "Looky thar' will ya! Our' l'il red friend likes it, he sho'ly do. He be a singin' to' da' Lord!" Automatically, Ben turned into the direction the voice had come from and with elation entering his heart, he curiously gasped, "Fred?"

His heart sunk within his chest as he remembered the accident and somberly realized that Fred wasn't there and he had just imagined hearing his voice. The cardinal's song chimed again and then he spotted the crimson soloist sitting on the rail of a white gazebo, just fifteen feet away in the snow. Normally Ben loved to hear cardinals sing, but today it gave him a peculiarly eerie sensation. It wasn't so much the singing that bothered him however, it was hearing or imagining the voice of his departed friend. The words Ben thought he heard just moments ago, actually had been said, amazingly or hauntingly, according to how one would choose to view the phenomenon, on this very spot over two and a half years ago.

Ben stared sullenly at the cardinal as it continued to sing. "Lord, what's wrong with me?" He silently asked as he raised his eyes and peered past the gazebo, at the one area of the church's property, he had purposely avoided looking at all morning, the cemetery. Even now he tried to resist the overwhelming lure that directed his gaze at the one snow covered hump in the snow that formed Fred's grave. Sadness started to settle around Ben like a misty blanket, trying to envelop him in misery and a bone-chilling shiver coursed through his body.

He got back in the truck, turned the heat on full blast thinking, "Don't go there, Ben! Don't do this to yourself!" He rolled his window down a bit, just enough to hear the cardinal who was still joyfully singing. Trying desperately to enjoy the beautiful song and the sharp, beautiful contrast of the bird's brilliant red coat against the snow covered gazebo, he forced his focus away from the cemetery. Trying to appreciate the white landscape, the blue sky overhead and the sunshine streaming through the windshield, while at the same time, reminding himself that it was Christmas Eve, Ben forced a wry smile. "Lord, am I going nuts," He questioned aloud as grief seemed to be just mere inches away, pouding on the door of his heart screaming, "Let me in!"

The cardinal whistled again and Ben remembered Fred's words, "He be a singin' fer da' Lord!" A rendition of, "We Three Kings of Orient Are," began playing on the radio as a tear formed in Ben's left eye. Ever so slowly, it slid down his cheek as he sat looking at the gazebo. His mind was drifting back again, to another seemingly nice, beautiful and fair-weathered day. Ben tensed up, fearing that he would soon be falling victim to his emotions once more. He kept telling himself, "Come on Ben!... Think good thoughts!... Good thoughts!... You can do it!" Closing his eyes he kept repeating, "Good thoughts!... Good thou...!"

CHAPTER TEN

"Ouch! Why You... You!" Five pairs of eyes glanced up as the exclamation of pain echoed in the church yard. "Go ahead, let her rip Pastor Rick! We understand, and we wouldn't tell no one, would we boys?" Prodded Dave Wilson as he turned to look at his co-workers with a devilish gleam and a wink. Everyone wanted to laugh, but they didn't because they understood how bad it had to of hurt. Each of them knew how Pastor Rick felt, for they too had fallen victim, to the painful striking of the wrong nail with a hammer before. For most of them however, restraint from the use of profanity wasn't their first thought, and at least one of them had appeared to develop a whole new four-letter-word language the last time he smashed his own thumb. The thing that really had the men biting their tongues to keep from showboating their amusement however, was the fact that Pastor Rick hadn't struck his finger just once that day, not even twice, but actually three painfully excruciating times.

Ben chuckled as he remembered how he had stood up straight on his ladder holding his black and blue, freshly bloodied and throbbing thumb as he rolled his eyes heavenward. Then composing himself he offered up an oration as if he were in his pulpit and it was Sunday morning, instead of Saturday. "Gentlemen, I must confess, that the temptation to verbally sin is rather appealing at this precise moment, but I shall not curse.

I shall however, draw my strength from the Lord." Spreading his arms wide as if to encompass the small group of builders he continued, "Fellow carpenters, far be it from me as the shepherd entrusted to this meager flock of the Lord's workers, I shall not succumb to the devils provocation, thus setting a bad example for the rest of you poor, misguided sinners." At this he started grinning and he added with a flourish, "I must deny however, the validity of the well known assertation claiming that the third time is a charm, for believe me when I tell you, my thumb just plain hurts."

Everyone laughed, but not near as heartily as they did after Fred suggested in his deep voice, "Did ya' e'er think Pasta' Rick, thet' perhaps it hurts something' awful jest' ta' reminds ya' thet yer one of us poor, misguided sinners too?" Dave, a fifty two year old mechanic suddenly whooped and exclaimed, "Why fella's, Ole Fred's right! I'll be hog-tied and tickled pink, Pastor Rick, really is just one of us after all! And to think that I thought he was a goody-two-shoed alter boy from way back." Pastor Rick adopted the air of a kid caught with his hand in the cookie jar as he countered, "Yes, of course. I must admit that it is true, I really am one of you." Then hanging his head as if shamed, he added, "I just wish being one of you didn't have to be so absurdly painful!"

Ben grinned at Pastor Rick across the top of the new gazebo they were building for the church as the rest of their group chuckled. It was a sunny June morning with just a slight breeze blowing and a few white tufts of cotton drifting across a radiant blue sky. A robin hopped across the ground nearby listening for worms while an array of songbirds serenaded the men from around the church property. Honey bees and butterflies flitted across the lawn and the sound of Pastor Rick's boys playing with their dog, Jeeters, could be heard coming from the direction of the parsonage as it mingled with the sound of hammers and saws busy at work.

A small open shelter amidst a flower garden, had been the idea of the church council to provide a place of beauty and solitude for people visiting the cemetery or just those individuals desiring to sit back, relax and enjoy the outdoors. Thirty five year old Mark Sefton, a carpenter by trade had been solicited by the council to head up the project. He and his thirteen year old son Zach, along with Pastor Rick, Ben, Fred and Dave had spent the last few Saturdays making the dream a reality. Pastor Rick, Ben and Mark were on ladders applying cedar shakes to the roof while Fred, Dave and Zach, with an I-Pod at his side and a bud in his ear, were painting the posts, railings and seats. Dave tried poking a little fun at Zach, who proved himself to be a worthy adversary, dishing it back at him equally. By noon the roof was done and most of the painting, except for the gazebo's floor.

Ben didn't know how the other men felt, but he was so hungry that his stomach was sending out an S.O.S. fearing that his mouth had been kidnapped. They had started early, at 6:00 a.m. and so not wanting to awaken Sarah by making too much noise in the kitchen, he just had nabbed a coffee and a sausage and egg sandwhich at, "Just like Ma's" on the way to the church, for breakfast. At about 9:00 a.m. Dave and Mark's wives showed up at the church to inspect the men's work and bring them two dozen assorted sinkers from the "Donut Stop" in town along with coffee, milk and juice. Pastor Rick, Ben, Dave and Mark each had three of the delicious treats while Fred and Zach devoured the remaining dozen. Dave harassed both of them by making pig-like noises while they ate, and the rest of the fella's really did wonder where the two donut munchers could possibly be putting it all. Much like Fred, Zack was skinny as a rail, but full of vim and vigor. Pastor Rick even went as far with his curiosity to say to Fred, "Fred? I can understand Zach's appetite, because after all, he's a growing boy you know. What I can't fathom is how come you don't weigh at least three hundred pounds, because I've seen you eat like this before. Where in heaven's good name do you put it all?"

Fred just looked at Pastor Rick for a few seconds, smiled and slowly answered, "Wal' ah' reckon ah' jest packs it into muh' python's." With a puzzled look, Pastor Rick asked, "Into your python's?" Ben nearly split a gut laughing when Fred pointed to each of his skinny biceps and drawled out, "Yesiree' Pasto' Rick. Ya see, ah' packs it here n' here." Then looking over at Zack, he asked, "Ain't it rawt, Zach?" Zack smiled widely, patting his own upper arms and replied, Yes Sir, Mr. Stone. It sure is! Donuts are the breakfast of real men." Everyone laughed and then Ben added, "If that's true, then I'll take another dozen of them chocolate, candy-sprinkled ones." That had been nearly three hours ago and Ben wasn't the only one ready to eat.

Sarah, Martha and Monica were in charge of lunch today, and as Ben stepped down off of his ladder, he was glad to see the ladies and Pastor Rick's boys, unloading the trunk of a car backed up to the edge of the parking lot. Soon, they approached with their arms full of what had to be delectable goodness. "Whooeeeee! Here come the vittles!" Dave exclaimed excitedly. Pastor Rick, Fred and Ben met their wives with a kiss, but when they offered to help the ladies with their burdens they were given, you guessed it, yet another version, of "The look," this one saying, "No chance, your hands are filthy." The tantalizing aromas which began wafting in the air smelled so good that they would have made a stone statue hungry and working on the gazebo was quickly forgotten.

There were two picnic tables off to one side of the gazebo. While the women set up for the meal, all six of the famished workers made haste across the parking lot, to wash their hands in the church's bathroom, their mouth's watering with the anxiety of devouring whatever culinary delights the ladies had brought. When they returned to the tables, they were not disappointed for the feast laid out before them, made them feel like they were kings.

After everyone was seated, Pastor Rick said a mercifully quick prayer and the women uncovered their dishes, enjoying the praises and looks of admiration they were receiving from the gazebo crew. Monica commenced to filling Eric and Jacob's plates as they took turns hitting one another in the shoulder. Martha and Sarah each had to resist the urge to fill Fred and Ben's plates as if they were children, and allow them to help themselves. Fred's eyes lit up big time, when Martha unveiled a bowl of her famous German potato salad, a bowl of green beans with baby potatoes, onions, and bacon mixed in and a big platter of honey-glazed barbequed boneless chicken wings.

Ben knew that Sarah had brought his favorite dessert, a super delicious, sweet, rich, creamy home-made chocolate pie, but he had no idea what she had brought for the meal. His stomach was ready to flip for joy, when she uncovered one of Ben and little Sammi's favorites, cheesy tater-tot casserole. She also had brought country style baked beans, homemade dill pickles, a fresh fruit tray and the sweetest cinnamon-butter rolls you ever sank your teeth into, and to top it off, they were still warm too!

Monica was no slouch when it came to cooking either. She had learned how to hold her own in the social competition of cooking for church gatherings. To her son's and husband's delight, she first uncovered her own special version of cheesy hotdogs wrapped in biscuits. Then she opened up some of the best vegetable soup anyone had ever tasted and she had made two desserts. One was a sinfully rich strawberry cheesecake and the second, a plate of ooey gooey, double-chocolate brownies drizzled with hot fudge and caramel. By the end of dessert the men would hardly be able to move, but man, was that feast Gooooood!

Half way through the meal, Jacob and Eric's dog, 'Jeeters' showed up with an appetite as big as the all outdoors. At the time, he was only about a year old, but already huge. When he first arrived, he went from person to person around the tables, rolling his big puppy dog eyes and begging, "Please give me something, anything!.... I'm starving here, can't you see!... Please Feed Me!"

Pastor Rick had exercised great patience and went to great lengths to teach Jeeters proper table manners. He was quite proud and would often boast about how well behaved the canine would act when people were eating. He hadn't been able to break the huge dog of begging, but he would only eat what was given to him. The women and most of the men were able to resist the woeful stare of the hungry mongrel, but Zach felt sorry for him. He gave in and tossed his, "Suddenly new best friend" a piece of a dinner roll. which disappeared faster than a hummingbird's wink. "Zachary Sefton, not at the table," his father warned. "Sorry Pop," was Zach's reply as he smiled at the big dog. Jeeters sat on his haunches next to Zack for two whole minutes, quietly begging for more until he finally realized that no more was to be had. He stopped in front of Mark next, who just looked at him and said, "No one is serving here," as the yearning eyes sadly looked up at him.

He then ambled alongside the table, looking for someone else too soft-hearted to resist his whiles. Past experience had taught Jeeters a thing or two about dining. He had learned which members of the church's congregation would feed him and who would not. He knew Pastor Rick and his wife would not, until they were done eating, so no use wasting time with them. The boys were always good for a bite or two, but they had spent the entire morning tugging on his ears, jumping on his back and playing "fetch" with him and he needed a break from them. As much as he loved both of them, he was still hoping to get some food from someone else for the moment, someone who wouldn't nearly jerk his ears off of his head.

As he made his way around the rest of the people at the tables he was thinking, "Ben and Sarah Chambers, naw they won't feed me and neither will that tricky Dave Wilson. Martha, well she's nice, but she won't feed me either, but wait. There's Fred, my favorite guy. He'll feed me because he's nice and he can't say no to me." Jeeters parked himself right next to Fred and put on the saddest face a dog could wear. Soon, everyone at the table was watching to see what Fred would do. Martha whispered, "Fred, you big softy, don't do it." Fred looked at the begging pooch, and then he glanced back at Martha who was slowly shaking her head to and fro. Then Jeeters turned on the charm as he began to whimper and poor Fred was in a quandary and didn't know what to do. Jeeters reached out with his paw and placed it in Fred's lap, whimpering louder. Inadvertently, Fred started reaching for a chicken wing on his plate and Martha gave him a stern look and hissed, "Fred!"

You could almost envision smoke rolling out of Fred's left ear as he struggled with decision. Suddenly, with his mind made up, he gulped, swallowing his Adam's apple as he said, "Sorry Dear," to Martha, and he handed a piece of chicken to the dog whom was more than graciously willing to accept his generous offering. Everyone burst out laughing, as Martha exclaimed, "Well, I never!" but soon, she was laughing as well. Ben couldn't help, but to admire his friend even more than he already did, for the immeasurable kindness in his heart. The dog made his way over to the two boys, got a few tidbits from them and then he took off to find a nice quiet spot in the sun to sleep before they could use him as a bucking bronco. By the time dessert was over, each of the men were also ready for a nap, but there was still work to be done. The younger boys took off to play while the women cleaned up the picnic area and the men and Zach got back to work. By 5:30 p.m. the gazebo was completed and everything was either put away or loaded back onto the truck it had came out of.

A white rock path made its way to and around the peaceful shelter and a colorful array of flowers, dotted with several waist high green bushes, all forming a beautiful garden, surrounded it. Ben and Fred volunteered to take care of watering the new plants and they insisted that the others go home to their families. When they were finished with the watering, they each grabbed a cold drink out of the parish hall's soda machine and went back out, sat at one of the picnic tables and admired the job they had done. Everyone had been well pleased and rightly so, the two men now observed, for it truly did look good.

"Ben?" said Fred as he crumpled up his quickly emptied soda can. "Yeah, what is it?" Ben asked. Fred stretched a bit and yawned big as he replied, "Ah' dunno bout ya'll, but ah's plumb t'ard." Ben could feel muscles aching that hadn't been used in a month of Sundays and he was starting to get stiff already. "I'm pretty well tuckered out myself, Buddy, but I feel good and we did great." Ben watched Fred nod in agreement and looking at his watch he added, "We'd best get going soon to go get cleaned up and take the girls out." Before he could move however, a bright red male cardinal suddenly alit on top of the gazebo and started singing his glorious song to the skies. Fred's eyes lit up and he stood up pointing at the new arrival, saying, "Looky thar' will ya! Our l'il red friend likes it, he sho'ly do. He be singin' to da' Lord!"

With those words echoing in Ben's mind as he sat in his truck on the freshly plowed church parking, his thoughts returned to the present and he smiled. Looking out at the cardinal who was still singing atop of the gazebo, he wondered if it possibly could be the same one Fred had observed. He turned the truck heater's fan down to low and he saw Jeeters go rambling by in front of his truck. The big dog neither looked left nor right as he plowed through the snow with his tongue hanging. It was as if he were in a world all his own, lost in his own thoughts and Ben could surely relate to that. He wondered if the big galoot knew about and perhaps even missed Fred too. After one last glance in the direction of Fred's grave, and a new onslaught of sadness hit Ben, he repeated what he had said so many times before, "God, it just not fair!" After a brief struggle with depression however, Ben decided that he was going to try to be happy this Christmas Eve, even if he did immensely miss his best friend.

Ben started humming, as his favorite version of "White Christmas," sung by the one man whose unique voice everyone recognizes, started playing from the radio. Although the voice on the airwaves wasn't as deep, it reminded Ben of Fred's melodic drone. Looking up towards the sky he whispered, "Merry Christmas Buddy!" The clock on the radio said it was ten minutes past noon.

Next to the radio and stuck to the face of the dashboard was a close-up picture of Sammi smiling from ear to ear and looking cross-eyed at a beautiful monarch butterfly which was resting on her little button nose. The photo reminded Ben that he was going to get to spend the afternoon with his favorite little girl and he was sure looking forward to it. He rolled up his window, glancing out at the cardinal one last time and put the truck in gear. Just before he could take off, his stomach groaned, letting him know that it was high time he sent some food down, for his internal fuel tank was running on empty. Then he felt a strange vibration against his chest. Quickly shifting back to park he thought, "What the... ?" until he heard the muffled tone of island music playing and he realized it was coming from his cell phone inside his coat's breast pocket. Sarah had found the ring tone already programmed into a small list of choices on Ben's phone. It was her hope that the jingle would help lift his spirits and give him happy thoughts, reminding him of the Caribbean cruise they had taken on their anniversary last year. Her idea was kind of working because right now while fumbling to get the phone out of several layers of clothing, he was also picturing the sparkling blue waters off of the coast of Jamaica.

"Your dime, my time." Ben answered after finally freeing the phone from his pocket and flipping it open. "Hey, Honey it's me. I finished all of my morning errands and we're at Amy's now. How's your playing in the snow, going?" Sarah's sweet voice was just what he needed to hear at the moment. Ben laughed and answered, "Oh you know me Dear, I just can't get enough. You should have been with me. I got to play at home, at Martha's, over to Old Man Shipley's and I just got done romping around over here at the church, with Pastor Rick's boys." Sarah took on a fake tone of seriousness as she said, "Oh, so you had all of that fun without me, while I was slaving away getting ready for Christmas, huh?" Knowing that she was just kidding, Ben returned, "Oh you had your chance to come, but too bad. You even missed out on some of Monica's homemade chocolate chip cookies." Sarah laughed on the other end as she said, "Honey, it's you whose missing out because Martha and I are over here at Amy's with her and a certain curly-topped cutie, that you just adore, making cookies and candy." Ben heard giggling in the background and excited squeals yelling, "It me PamPaw! It me!" Picturing a little bundle of energy with chocolate all over her face, he said, "Ask Sammi if she's ready to come play with her grandpa for a while." As she asked, Sarah must have held the phone to Sammi's mouth for her answer, because a piercing scream issued forth from the receiver that nearly broke his eardrum followed by, "Yaaaaaay! PamPaw come pway!" Sarah came back on the line laughing and said, "Ben, Dear, we're going to make one of your favorites for lunch, grilled cheese and tomato soup." At the mention of that delicious combination, Ben's stomach roared internally. Monica's cookies had been delicious, but they had done little to stifle the hunger of the ravenous beast that seemed to be rampaging within him. "I'll be there in about ten shakes of a lambs tail,... and Sarah," he added. "Yes Dear," she returned. Ben smiled to himself, as he replied, "I love you!" and he hung up.

He shifted into drive once more and just for kicks, he gunned the motor a little and twisted the wheel just hard enough to cause the back end of his truck to fishtail a bit. It gave him an undeniable sense of exhilaration and he felt more alive than he had in months. Right now he wasn't giving Fred a single thought. His entire focus was on what he needed to do this afternoon, eating good food and having fun with Sammi. "Let it Snow" blared on the radio and Ben sang along, if you could call his caterwauling, singing, as he pulled out of the parking lot and headed off toward Amy's.

CHAPTER ELEVEN

"It Woodoff PamPaw!... Wisen',... It Woodoff!" Sammi joyfully exclaimed from her car seat as she squirmed, frantically pointing at the truck's radio. "It sure is!" Ben returned with a smile and together they sang about the red-nosed reindeer all the way to "Lawson's Deli." Lunch hadn't been fancy, but it sure hit the spot and the fresh, homemade cookies and fudge for dessert were as the teenagers would say, "da' bom!" The cab of Ben's truck smelled absolutely delicious because a tray of the cookies and candy along with a card holding ten dollars in it for Billy, the paperboy, lay on the floorboard under Sammi's dangling feet. Ben and Sammi were going to spend the afternoon at his house, but before they did, there were still a few things needing done and stops to make.

The mixed smells of spiced cider, smoked meat and cheddar cheese greeted the pair as they entered the store through a glass door which was covered with a holiday design done in spray-on snow. A steady flow of people were entering and exiting the building while salutations of, "Merry Christmas!" echoed all around. "Lawson's" was all decked out for the holidays, inside and out, with garland, lights and a star above the door. They had static cling yuletide characters on every window and a decorated tree near the meat counter with baskets of fresh fruit wrapped in red and green cellophane around its base. In one corner of the store a giant toy-filled stocking hung from the ceiling with a drawing entry box beneath it full of the names of hopeful children. Just inside the door was a big metal washtub on a stand full of free peanuts in the shell with a big cardboard Santa standing behind it. "I just love this place." Ben thought as he grabbed some peanuts, shelled them and asked Sammi if she wanted any. Acting shy, which was rare for her and not letting go of his coat tail she smiled and nodded. Her beautifully bright, wide eyes sparkled with wonder as she looked all about the store.

It's safe to say that "Lawson's Deli" wasn't just your run-of-the-mill butcher shop. Oh sure, they had their processing area and freezers out behind the meat counter, but they also had a fresh-made sandwich counter and a soda fountain with several tables set up for any hungry diners who wished to eat there.

There were five, four foot tall aisles of various items running down the center of the store displaying everything from canned goods, medical supplies, holiday decorations, hardware and automotive goods to a surpisingly vast array of Christmas gift ideas, candy and greeting cards. One wall was covered with metal signs and sports memorabilia celebrating the town's many generations of school athletes and the career of a home-town boy who hit it big in the "Major's." The opposite wall displayed a huge collage of business cards, "For Sale" and "Wanted" ads, newspaper clippings, and photographs covering local hunting, fishing, farming, general history, and anything else the customers deemed of importance enough to post it there.

There was a dairy section with locally produced milk, eggs, butter, blocks of cheese and "Lawson's" own, rich, creamy vanilla soft-serve ice cream. For the holiday they had added a little peppermint flavoring to the mix and today a pretty, young woman who worked there, whose name tag read, "Heather" was handing out free baby-sized cones. The first was so good, Ben and Sammi couldn't resist going back for another. There was a donut counter, a fresh produce section and in a room off to one side was a room full of hunting and fishing supplies. There were mountings on the walls of that room with more pictures of the local residents outdoor successes and even Ben and Fred's smiling mugs could even be found in there. One such example was a picture of them struggling to hold a gigantic catfish they had pulled out of a quarry pond North of town. After a quick friendly dispute over mounting the fish, and Ben's finally relenting to just taking a picture of it to prove bragging rights, they had thrown the monster back into the depths it had come from. Every time Sammi came to the store with Ben, she wanted to see that picture and today was no exception, for she was now tugging his coat into that direction, pointing and saying, "Big fis' PamPaw! Wet's go see big fis!" Ben just laughed as he let her lead the way.

"PamPaw, Fwed, and b-i-i-i-i-g fis'," Sammi uttered, while pointing at each image in the picture while he held her up to see it. As Ben looked at Fred in the picture, a pang of sorrow washed through him, but forcing a smile as he sat Sammi back down on her feet, he tickled her saying, "All right Princess, you've seen the big fish. Now, lets go get what we came for and I'll bet I know what you want, Cigar's!" Sammi's sparkling green eyes flashed with anticipation and excitement as she squealed, "No Pampaw, you silwy', I wan' S-s-s-s-mokies!" If there is anything "Lawson's" is even more famous for than their soft-serve, it is their smoked beef sticks and no trip there would be complete without getting some. Sammi nearly drug Ben back into the main store and she started to throw a fit when they had to take their place in the long line which was wrapped nearly half way around the store.

Oh yes, Ben's precious little grand-daughter may appear to be an angel most of the time, but you'd better believe that the devil's horns sometimes hide just below the surface of her dark curls and on occasion, they have the tendency to show themselves at the drop of a hat. Fortunately today however, a gentle warning of, "You'd better be good Little Girl if you want, "You Know Who," to come tonight." Sammi slowly unclenched her tiny fists, the frown left her face and would you believe it, the sudden tears even stopped miraculously as she transformed back into the innocent little darling everyone so loved. Then she yelled with excitement, "Sanna' Caus'! Yaaaaaaaaay!"

The line moved rather quickly and in no time they were in front of the coolers beside the register. In front of the meat counter on a low shelf were jars of home-canned fruits, veggies, jams and sauces and behind the glass, the leanest and freshest cuts of meat you ever set your sights on, waited to be purchased. Next was a section of various cheeses and then three rows of sliced cheese and sausage trays with little colored bows and nametags on top. "There's ours, Sammi," Ben said pointing at two in the back row. She smiled and cheered, "Yummmmmmmy!"

At the register, Peggy Lawson greeted them with a cheery, "Merry Christmas Ben! Who is that pretty little elf beside you there,... oh,... why it's Sammi. Merry Christmas Sweetie!" Sammi half hid behind Ben's leg blushing as he smiled and said, "Merry Christmas Peggy! You guys are sure busy today, but that's good, right?" Suddenly, Frank, Peggy's husband's voice, belted out from behind him, "Busy is absolutely Grrreeeeat! Merry Christmas Ben, I've got your order right here." Frank clapped Ben on the shoulder and he leaned down and winked at Sammi just before stepping around Peggy and grabbing the cheese and sausage trays bearing the "Chambers" name and putting them on the counter next to his wife. She rung them up asking Ben if there would be anything else and Sammi forgot her temporary shyness and belted out, "Smokies!"

Moments later, Ben and Sammi found themselves over at the big stocking, putting Sammi's name into the drawing. Then they marched proudly out of "Lawson's Deli" with their purchases and each of them had a smoked beef stick clenched in their teeth and two more were sticking up out of Ben's breast pocket for the ride home. Ben put Sammi in her car seat and closed her door, and he had just opened the driver's side door when a familiar voice rang out, "Hey Ben! Ben Chambers! Wait up a minute!"

He turned to see Nathan Shipley coming as fast as he could hobble with a three-toed cane from the direction of "Lawson's" front door, with a fruit basket nestled in the crook of his free arm. It was his driveway that Ben had cleared this morning. Mr. Shipley was a ninety-seven year old widower and retiree from the same plant Ben had worked at. He was still sharp as a tack, but his body would no longer let him do what he once had. Ben, Fred, and several others from the church, often helped him with little projects around his house. The older gentleman walked up, breathing hard and handed the fruit basket to Ben saying in a raspy voice, "Merry Christmas Ben!" Ben took the basket with one hand and shook Mr. Shipley's hand with the other as he replied, "Why Merry Christmas Mr. Shipley, but what's this?" While still holding Ben's hand, Nathan bent to the side, looking around him and looked at Sammi sitting in the truck. He said, "Merry Christmas you Cutie!" Sammi just grinned from her seat giving a little wave as Mr. Shipley straightened back up, and looking Ben in the eyes with a glint of humor, he sarcastically said, "Why, it's a new car of course. Ain't you ever seen a fruit basket before?" Ben laughed ironically and countered, "Why of course I can see that it's a fruit basket, but why are you giving it to me?" The old man let go of Ben's hand, readjusted his cane and scratched his chin before he answered, "My Gracie, bless her soul. She was the one taught me all about givin'. I surely do miss her, but I reckon I'll be joining her up yonder soon, one of these days. Anyway, this is my Christmas present to you and your family, so Merry Christmas!" Ben turned putting the basket on the seat next to Sammi's car seat and then he turned back feeling a little guilty as he said, "Thank you Nathan, but I kind of feel bad because I didn't get you anything."

The older man cleared his throat and replied, "Ben, you gave me your gift this mawnin', by doing my drive and when you wouldn't take nothing fer' it, I got to thinking' bout' all of the things you do and I wanted to give you a token of my appreciation, so there it be. I was fixin' to take it by your house, but then I saw you and that little angel there in yer' truck, ahead of me in the line back there, (he hooked a thumb and gestured back over his shoulder) in 'Lawson's.' I'm just glad I caught you, before you skedaddled." The two men exchanged another handshake and parted with another, "Merry Christmas!" As Ben started up the truck, Sammi asked, "PamPaw, who dat?" As he watched Mr. Shipley hobble away, Ben felt sorry for him, wondering how he dealt with the holidays, with his wife gone. He said, "Princess, that was Mr. Nathan Shipley and he's a wonderful old man that goes to our church." Sammi grinned saying, "I wike' him!" Ben felt warm inside as he smiled at her and replied, "Me too Honey, me too!"

"Oh, you better watch out! You better not...!" Ben pointed at Sammi as they sang along with the radio. In the seat, up against the fruit basket, the red leaves of a poinsettia, they bought at the flower shop for Sarah, seemed to bounce in rhythm to the music. Sammi had said she was thirsty so they went through a fast-food drive-thru for sodas and had one more stop to make before going home. The roads were completely clear of snow now and the traffic was heavy for a small town and newly constructed snowmen seemed to be waving from every other yard. The song ended and a meteorologist came on the air forecasting one to three more inches of snow this evening. Yaaaayyyy snow," Sammi said excitedly. Ben agreed with a smile and a nod.

When they were about two blocks from their stop, and just half a mile from home, Sammi was busy looking out the window and Ben was going through a list in his mind to see if he'd forgotten anything he needed to do today, when, "Whop!" A big snowball came flying from out of nowhere and smashed into the windshield. Sammi screamed and started sniffling and Ben even jumped before flipping on the wipers to whisk away the loose powder now splattered in front of him. "Don't worry Honey, it was just a snowball." he said calmly, trying to comfort Sammi as he looked in his mirror to see if he could determine where the winter-time missile had launched from.

Behind him on the left he could see a bunch of boys running to hide and one of them looked strangely familiar. Then recognition kicked in and Ben honked his horn twice. He flipped on his right blinker, slowed down and said to Sammi, "Why it's Billy, just the guy I was looking for." She just looked at him like he had two heads, stopped sniffling and started singing, "Away in a Manger" with the radio.

Ben turned his truck around in a driveway and headed back to where all of the boys had disappeared except for Billy. Ben passed the boy, honking and pointing to the next drive where he pulled in and opened his door. "I'll be right back Sammi," he said and getting out of the truck, he closed the door and walked to the passenger side door and waited for Billy to slowly approach. Billy had his head down and drug his feet as if scared so Ben said, "Billy, hurry up and come over here for a minute, I need to talk to you." Billy sauntered up to Ben stammering for words as he wrung his hands and said, "Hey, a,... Mr.... Chambers. I'm sor... sorry about that snowball Dean threw. He was trying to hit me and...and...!"

Ben looked sternly at Billy for a full ten seconds without saying a word, drawing out the moment for the poor boy just to be ornery. Then, still not smiling and with a level tone he opened the passenger door of the truck, looked in, winking and grinning at Sammi and said, "Billy, I'll tell you what," Billy cringed as if he were going to get hit, and Ben let him have it. Not with harsh words or punishment like Billy half-expected, but with kindness and generosity. Immediately upon recognizing Billy in the group of fleeing boys, Ben had forgotten about the snowball and focused on why he was in this neighborhood in the first place. He grabbed the cookie and candy tray and card off of the floorboard and said, "About that there snowball." Then turning to his nervous paperboy he smiled, holding out the gift and said, "Forget it and just be glad Dean has bad aim. Merry Christmas Billy, and thanks for the great job you always do delivering our newspaper."

Billy's eyes nearly bulged out of his head and a look of relief washed over his face as he accepted the gift. He was at a loss for words as he fumbled to get his gloves off and open up the card. His eyes lit up again as the wind nearly snatched the ten dollar bill folded up inside and after he read the card he looked up with a big smile and said, "Gee thanks Mr. Chambers!" Ben reached out and shook Billy's hand saying, "You're quite welcome young man. Mrs. Chambers made them cookies and candy, and you're lucky I saw you when I did, or I might of eaten them." Billy looked at the tray, through the green plastic wrap and Ben swore he licked his lips. Looking up the boy said,

"Thanks again Mr. Chambers and please thank your wife for me." Ben turned away smiling and saying, "I will Billy! You and your family have a Merry Christmas!" He got back in his truck and made a funny face at Sammi who giggled in return. After backing out onto the road, and as he pulled away, he looked in the mirror once more. Some of Billy's friends, had come out of hiding and were walking cautiously up to him and Ben smiled because he knew they were all going to have chocolate on their faces very soon.

CHAPTER TWELVE

"Joy to the World," concluded on the radio as Ben and Sammi pulled into the driveway. A squirrel whom was playing on the shed roof disappeared at the sight of the truck and startled a trio of sparrows as he made his hasty departure. As he put the truck in "Park," Ben nudged Sammi and pointed up to the shed's cupola. A smile lit up her face as she saw a pair of mourning doves perched high atop of its roof. Ben unbuckled and got out, noticing that the temperature was starting to drop a little. He went into the shed and swung open the big doors. After pulling the truck inside and closing the swinging doors he turned on the shed light just in time to see not one, but this time, two, cute mice bolt from the birdseed bin. "I've got to get a cat," Ben thought with a wry shake of his head. Then, he walked up to the passenger door of the truck and knocked on the window, smiling and waving at Sammi. As he opened the door and unbuckled her, she squealed, "I wanna make snow anel's PamPaw! Pweeeze!" Ben replied, "Okay Princess, you can make snow angels, but you have to stay close beside the shed, okay?" Sammie nodded her reply as he put on her hat and gloves.

As Ben lifted her out of the seat, the button on his coat sleeve hooked the glove compartment door and popped it open. He heard something thud to the floorboard, but didn't see what it was. Ben swung Sammi around and before her little feet could even touch the ground, her legs were moving and in a flash she was out the side door yelling, "Snow anel's, Yaaaay!" Ben walked over and looked out the door, breaking into laughter at the sight before him. He felt his heart swelling with love for the little cutie in jeans and a pink coat with matching gloves, hat and even boots, whom was laying on her back in the snow, wildly flailing her arms and legs back and forth. Particles of snow where spraying all around her, much like the water flying off of the back of a big dog shaking off after a bath. "I wish I had the camcorder right now," Ben silently surmised as he watched his granddaughter having the time of her life.

A few minutes later he spun around and walked back to the open door of the truck to get the fruit basket, the cheese and sausage trays, and the poinsettia. He also intended to put whatever had fallen out of the glove box back in it. Looking at the floorboard, Ben was puzzled for there lay a very old book of some sorts with a faded, worn and stained leather cover. "It looks like somebody's journal," Ben thought as he picked it up and two legal-sized white envelopes fell out and landed on the truck's seat. Ben looked down at the envelopes and nearly dropped the book as he stood stunned and unable to move for a few seconds. Right there on the top envelope, boldly staring up at him was his own name scrawled out in the handwriting of his dear departed friend, Fred. The second envelope was similarly addressed to Martha.

Ben's heart raced, his lower lip trembled and his hands shook like he was an archaeologist's who has just realized that he may have just unearthed some sacred scroll, as he reached for the envelopes and uttered, "What the... ?" Suddenly Ben focus was torn away when he felt someone pull at his coat. It was Sammi all covered with snow and she yelled with an excited voice, "Come see PamPaw!... Come see my anels!... Come see, pweese!"

Ben closed the glove compartment door, put the envelopes back in the journal and stuck it under his arm. "Go ahead Honey, I'll be right there," He said to Sammi who replied, "Okay PamPaw," and she was gone again. Then he stacked the cheese and sausage trays and carefully sat the fruit basket and poinsettia on top and managed to pick it all up without dropping a thing. He turned using his back-side to shut the truck door and out of the corner of his eye he saw another mouse dart across his workbench. As he left the shed, he nudged the light switch to "off," with his elbow, carefully spun around and tediously worked two fingers free to twist the doorknob's lock and pull the door shut. He was surprised that he managed it without dropping a thing. "Hey, I'm pretty good." Ben thought to himself as he turned to watch Sammi thrashing again with delight in the snow. "That's sure a pretty angel!" he hollered at her. Then he added, "Sammi, Honey. I'm going to take this stuff in the house and I'll be right back, okay?" He figured she was too busy having fun to even hear him, but surprisingly she replied, "Okay PamPaw!"

Less than four minutes later he was back watching Sammi and as it was definitely getting colder because Ben could see his breath on the air. Thanks to a little table by the back door of the house, he had gotten everything inside safely with no accidental mishaps. The cheese and sausage trays were in the fridge, the poinsettia was hidden in the master bedroom's bathroom to surprise Sarah later and the fruit basket was on the kitchen counter. Now, Ben wanted more than anything to look at the journal and curiosity was nearly eating him alive. Sammi was about due for a nap, so he contented himself with the knowledge that he'd get his chance soon, so he put the journal in the top drawer of his desk in the study. He decided he would however, read whatever was inside the envelope addressed to him right away. He grabbed it and quickly headed out to his snow-angel-making Princess. This time she was too busy pumping her arms and legs to notice his return, so he took advantage of her playtime to open the envelope and removed the note inside with his hands shaking uncontrollably. With a great effort of will he steadied himself, took a deep breath and looked up towards Heaven and asked, "Okay, what have you got to say to me, Buddy?"

Ben felt his heart racing like a trip-hammer as he slowly unfolded the letter. He glanced at the first page and was immediately impressed with the neatness, penmanship and the poetic flair with which it had been written. It seemed strange at first to have been written by a man whom usually opted to speak with a slow country drawl, but Ben knew that Fred could also speak as a man of education when he had felt the need to do so. For some crazy reason he remembered part of a famous animated movie he and Sarah had watched with Sammi one time. The main character, a big green fellow, was stating that he was like an onion, because he had many layers. Ben curiously thought to himself, "Fred was a man of many layers too." He felt a weird, indescribable sensation settle over him as he began to read and he imagined he could hear Fred's deep voice speaking to him.

28 September 2006,

My Dearest Friend, Ben,

If you find yourself reading this correspondence, than my intuitions have thus proven to be true;
And I am not quite at all, sure as what to do.

I have been experiencing the strangest feelings, of knowing as of late;
That I shall be called into the presence of our Creator soon for an appointment that will not wait.

I find myself scared, worried, but strangely excited too;
This venture is one which I have steadily traveled ever since that Christmas Eve in 1972.

That was a time when all hope was lost and I had drifted much too far from God and was doomed unto a most frightfully bitter end;
It was then that my Lord Jesus lifted me up and you Benjamin Chambers, became my closest friend.

It is because you are my friend that I ask of you a favor, if you will;

One that sadly, I myself will be unable to fulfill.

I know that my precious Martha will be forever heart-broken when I go;
However you and Sarah will watch after her, in my heart, this I know.

She will stand tough for all the world to see, but inside she will be crying as she yearns for me;
She loves the Lord Jesus with all of her heart, but she will not understand, unless you can help her to believe, and then to see.

That we will never truly be apart;
As long as she keeps me inside of her heart.

For all of us believer's, this life and death here on Earth, are just part of God's grand plan;
I'm not telling her goodbye, but just 'See you later!' until when in Heaven, we shall meet again.

Ben, go ahead and read my journal, and of my life, you will gain a new insight;
But, please, give it to Martha when she needs it most, you will know when the time is right.

Today I retired from the plant and tomorrow, who knows, we may fish;
But when I am called and Jesus beckons me home, here is my last wish.

May you all Live, Love, Laugh and Rejoice and after a while, no longer grieve;
For it is on a happy of note, that I much prefer to leave.

With the angels I may soon sing;
Loud hosannas to the Lord our King.

*Believe that a star shining high ion the sky, like the one
which should adorn every Christmas tree;
Once led to Jesus, and thus he saved everyone, including
you and me.*

*Until we meet again in Heaven's glorious realm, one day;
I shall always be, but a thought away.*

Your Friend Forever,

Frederick Flint Stone

A solitary tear rolled down Ben's cheek as he slowly looked
up from the paper, not exactly sure how he was feeling at the
moment. He refolded the letter and stuck it back in its envelope
and in his pocket. Trying to picture Fred in Heaven was the easy
part, but convincing himself that everything was truly okay, was
a horse of a different color. The letter should've made him feel
better, but sadly, it had quite the opposite effect.

It took a monumental effort for Ben to stave off the sudden
attack of distraught emotions now threatening to unsettle his
nerve. He honestly and desperately feared that he was near to
falling off of the brink and into the abyss of eternal depression.

Inside his mind, he kept telling himself, "Snap out of it
Ben! It's Christmas Eve, so be happy! Fred's in Heaven and
he wouldn't want you to do this to yourself! You're not doing
anybody any good! Toughen up and get control of yourself
man!" The internal battle raging within Ben, between what he
tried to convince himself he should be feeling, verses how he
really did feel, was more like as if he were a mouse stuck in a
maze of dead ends. He didn't know what to do and he felt like
bawling his eyes out.

"Help me God!" he desperately prayed as he began to relin-
quish his will-power and succumb to being trapped, slowly
losing himself in a horrifying labyrinth of emotional confusion.
"Oh Lord save me," he cried out again internally. He became
aware that something seemed to be pulling him down and he

could hear a muffled voice. Suddenly, his thoughts cleared and the fear and the pain subsided, leaving Ben confused. Again he felt the tug, but he noticed that it was at his coat sleeve this time. Once more he heard a voice, and great relief washed over him as he recognized that it was little Sammi's sweet and tender call, beckoning him back to reality. As he looked down into the sparkling green eyes of his granddaughter, love filled his heart.

"I co'd PamPaw, wet's' go in! I co'd," Sammi pleaded as she tugged at his sleeve. She looked worn out and was beginning to shake with cold. It also didn't help that she was covered from head to toe with snow. Ben shivered too, realizing that the temperature definitely had dropped some more. Ben dusted her off and scooped her up into his arms. He kissed her rosy cheeks as he surveyed the dozen or so mini-sized snow angels in the yard. "Your angels look great, Princess," he said as a stiff cold breeze made both of them shiver again. Ben rolled back his sleeve and looked at his watch. It was almost three o'clock and the sun was already getting low in the western sky. It was strangely quiet in the yard except for the occasional, wind generated rustle of dry, brown leaves still clinging to the trees branches. The steady "Drip!" "Drip!" "Drip," of water drops plunging off of the ends of the icicles hanging from the eaves of the house and shed sounded strange in the calm which seemed to have enveloped the world.

The birds and squirrels that usually frequented the yard were nowhere to be seen and the only life that seemed to exist, other than Ben and Sammi, was the occasional car that went coasting by out front. Sammi yawned really big, making it apparent that she was nearly ready for her nap-time. She nestled up tighter against Ben's chest she uttered, "PamPaw, I co'd n' tursty'."

Hugging his bundle of love tightly he said, "I'm cold and thirsty too, Sweetheart. I'll bet you're a little tired too, maybe ready for your nap, huh?" Sammi shook her head too and fro as she yawned again, while saying, "uh, uh. I not tawd' PamPaw."

Ben laughed as he said, "Well, I am." and then he suggested, "What do you say, we go in and have some hot chocolate and cookies. Then you can take your nap, okay?"

Sammi leaned back responding, "Hot chocowat an' cooooookies, Yaaaay," and inside they went.

"Whrrrrrrr DINGGGGG!!!" As the microwave shut off, Ben removed the two cups of steaming water and then sat on a bar stool at the kitchen counter next to Sammi. Her eyes grew big as he stirred in the powdery sweet and succulent mixture. Soon, the sweet aroma of warm chocolate filled her nostrils. He tested Sammi's cup to make sure that it wasn't too hot and just as he started to hand her the cup, he decided to tease her, after all that's what grandpa is supposed to do, right? He put on his best begger's look and asked, "Hey Princess, can I have your marshmallows, pleeeeeaasse?" Ben nearly fell off of his stool in amusement when Sammi gave him her own little variation of, "The Look," and replied, "Get weel', PamPaw!"

Ben and Sammi talked about her angel part in the church program tonight, about Christmas presents, Jesus, and a whole passel of other things while they ate cookies and drank the hot chocolate. By the time they were done, Sammi was too tired to resist as Ben took her to her room and tucked her under the covers for her afternoon nap. After kissing his sleepy princess on the forehead he went to his coat and retrieved Fred's note and then proceeded to the study to get the journal. Ben truly enjoyed the time he had spent with Sammi this afternoon, but ever since Fred's journal had fallen out of the glove compartment, he couldn't shake the burning curiosity of finding out what was in recorded within in its pages. He walked into the living room and stood before the Christmas tree looking up at the star on top without really seeing it. He was going over Fred's letter in his mind and wondering what his friend had meant when he wrote that Ben would know when the time was right, to give the journal to Martha. How could he possibly know the right time and help her, when thus far, he hadn't even come to terms with Fred's death, himself? He still wanted, no, he actually needed, some answers too, but oddly, he just didn't really didn't know what the questions were. "How many times have other people been as confused and lost as I am," he asked himself quietly.

When he could come up with now satisfying answer he just sighed, saying, "God, it's just not fair!"

Ben hoped that he would somehow find the miracle solution for the dilemma he was experiencing in the yellowed pages of the old journal. The clock on the fireplace mantle said that it was just shy of three-thirty which gave Ben an hour before he had to wake Sammi, take her back home and pick up Martha. It wasn't much time to read, but turning on a lamp and sitting in his recliner with his feet outstretched, Ben was determined to get started. He struggled for a moment, feeling strange and almost afraid to venture forth. He felt like he was on the verge of changing from an invited friend, into a intruder, as he braced himself to embark upon the journey into the private realms of Fred's life. The sudden urge to just close the journal and rush it over to Martha right now crossed Ben's mind, but at the same time, he knew that he had to read it first.

The first page was stained with a much faded, but still legible inscription which read;

12 May 1966,

This journal, presented to the greatest son, two parents could ever hope for. Always trust in the Lord, come home safe and remember that we love you very much! We are so proud of you, Private Stone!
Love, Mom & Dad

Ben had never known much about Fred's parents, but after reading that one small paragraph, it became quickly apparent that they had loved their son. Judging by the character of his friend, he knew that they must have been wonderful people. His hands were shaking as he carefully turned the brittle presentation page to see what entries lay beyond. A quick scan through the next several pages showed that Fred hadn't made daily entries as in a diary, but rather just a recording of the events he personally had found significant enough to record, starting with his time in Vietnam. Ben braced himself, for he knew that in visiting this integral part of his friends past, that it would most likely awaken in himself, a time he'd tried desperately many years ago, to forget.

There had been some good times over there, but they vastly paled in comparison to the awful memories, the things he had shared with no one, not at least since the terrible dreams had finally stopped. He desperately hoped to find some sense of closure hidden between the covers of the journal, so taking a deep breath, he started reading the pages containing the personal memoirs of his deceased best friend. Would the journal only paint a picture of a gentle, small, and average man with a giant voice, or would it give new insight to a remarkable child of God? It was obvious that he had been a wonderful husband and an extraordinary friend, but what unknown secrets would the old yellowed pages reveal, about the life of the man everyone had known as, "Frederick Flint Stone?"

CHAPTER THIRTEEN

4 November 1968,

It is a unusually odd Monday and with my first entry, I curiously find that I must question myself as to my presence in this Army camp, stuck somewhere deep inside of this absurd place they call Vietnam. Though I arrived not alone, I must confess that I find myself subdued into silent contemplation wondering and asking the Lord, if I have made the right decision. Six of my "Comrades in Arms" from "Boot Camp" have arrived with me and I wonder, "Are they thinking much the same as I?" When our plane landed two hours ago it was still dark and this place was a mystery. Even though it was early, we were openly excited, inwardly a little bit scared and at the same instance, proud to be "In Country." We were convinced that we would undoubtedly be the group of heroes who could help spread democracy and bring peace to a people, whom are hurting and being persecuted.

The nauseating stench of spilled blood on the floor and the bullet holes in the sides of the chopper which brought us thus far, further assisted by the sights of a burnt out village with war-torn, deceased bodies strung out across the terrain as we flew over, has interjected some doubt into our noble intentions. Yet, I know that my companions and I are equally committed to the ideal, that victory and success will be ours. We will undoubtedly liberate the victimized people of South Vietnam from the evil atrocities they have had forced upon them. Why is it that we will do this? Because we are Americans of course!

As Ben sat in his recliner and viewed the war through Fred's words he could remember feeling many of the same feeling himself when he was there. Although he had been drafted, he went forth full of American patriotism and vowed to serve his God, country and fellowman the best way he knew how. To this very day, although Ben doesn't necessarily always agree with every military decision made on behalf of our great nation, he fully supports and respects out troups. Granted, that war is never a good thing, he is also well aware of the fact that it sadly, is often necessary, for the ensured safety of a nations people and for others abroad.

Ben is, has always been, and will always be, the kind of American who bleeds red, white, and blue. He acknowledges that every freedom, every luxury, and absolutely everything that we can choose to make a part of our lives, has made possible for us, not because of our own daily efforts, but because of the blood sacrifices made by others. In America, many of these opportunities and choices in life have been made possible through the sacrifices made by our brave soldiers, right from the very beginning our great nation. Ben would be the first to tell you however, that a better life and more choices made available through a blood sacrifice, didn't start with military conflict or "American History" it started with God. It began when His only Son died for the sins of all people on a cross many years ago, and He gave us the choice, of whether or not, to believe. Ben believes, but being human, just like the rest of us, he has his struggles to deal with. Over the last few months he has been fighting his own emotions, arguing with what his faith has taught him all of his life and refusing to accept any sense of right in Fred's being taken away. His mind wants everything to be okay, but his heart says that it is not, so perhaps, just maybe, the journal will help?

The next several entries were ones that Ben can all too well, relate too. As he reads them, old memories, which had lain dormant for over thirty years rapidly come to life within the realms of his mind once more as if they had occurred just last week.

Day 24 — 28 November 1968,
It is Thanksgiving and I am weary from battle. It has seemed like an eternity, since the awful day I first arrived at this place. I am thankful to have survived thus far, but am saddened that my friend 'Jersey' did not. I saw the wire, but not in time to call out a warning and he... At least he did not suffer. Mom and Dad, eat some turkey for me, okay?

Day 51 — 25 December 1968,
Merry Christmas Mom and Dad, I miss you! More difficult times, I have never known, but I pray, a year from now to be home. Parts of this place are amazingly beautiful, but the violence, terror, blood and fear ruin it all. Sometimes I fear that perhaps, God too, has written this place off. We lost "Foo-Man" a crazy but solid soldier from Jersey, last night in a fire-fight. He had a wife and a daughter back home, but that's all I know.

Day 102 — 14 February 1969,
Dad, it's crazy. We did not fight today, but "Preacher" is still gone. He was about my age and we called him that because his father is a Baptist minister back in Connecticut. At "Mail Call" he received a correspondence which he rapidly disappeared with. A few minutes later, everyone in the camp dove for cover in response to a sudden gunshot. It wasn't the enemy, it was "Preacher." We found the letter on the ground next to his body,... it was a 'Dear John'."

Day 242 — 4 July 1969,
I have failed to write for quite some time, for my mind has been in a quandary. How will I survive of this horrid place and do I honestly want to? Today is supposed to be Independence Day, but it is virtually impossible for me to feel free. I don't recognize myself these days and I am sickened by the number of lives I've seen destroyed. I find myself envious, rather than glad, for the soldiers who have survived long enough to serve their time and get to go home. I sometimes catch myself, now being the one who looks with disdain at the new soldiers coming in. They look like rosy-faced kids who have no business being here with us battle-hardened warriors, but then who am I, for I am the same age or just slightly older than they. I do not believe that I inwardly wish to be anti-social or unfriendly, but perhaps it is because I do not want to get to know them . I have no desire to like them, just to watch them die later. Yet, at the same time, most of us here would, without a moments hesitation, sacrifice ourselves to save the life of any of our fellow soldiers. Mom… Dad? If you ever read this, do not fret and please just bear with my moment of woeful self-pity. Unlike those here who have chosen to turn to alcohol and drugs to deal with the war, I shall not. You have taught me to trust in the Lord, and through Him I shall persevere until the bitter end of this conflict, and I shall rejoin you and know real happiness once again.

Day 312 — 12 September 1969,
The last two days, will forever haunt the realms of my mind. In the morning, we found ourselves submersed deep in the heat of battle as we fought it out with the enemy in a swamp. We seemed to be outnumbered, and men dropping all around me like flies when Lt. Hinkle, a hard-nosed veteran of perhaps a whole twenty-three years of age, took a radio off of a dead soldier and successfully called in an air-strike. When the roar of the jets, the thick smoke and searing flames disappeared, so too, had the enemy.

We cautiously combed the swamp, searching for our wounded and fallen comrades. We were able to account for everyone, but 'Dallas' and 'Red' two of the last three of my buddies from 'Boot Camp'. We found what was left of them today in an abandoned enemy camp we discovered while on patrol. I am horrified and at a loss for adequate words to describe how my friends died and how very much they suffered before doing so. I now understand however, what it is to hate, for I truly hate my enemy. Yet I could never, ever bring myself to do such an evil as our heathen enemy has done.

Day 378 — 17 November 1969,
I am no longer confident that I shall one day leave this place. I was grazed by two bullets as I bent to check the pulse of Lt. Hinkle during a jungle fire-fight. He was dead and had been shot in the back of the head, an apparent victim of possible friendly-fire. He was supposed to return home this week. I have seen the best in some of my fellow soldiers, but sadly, more often than not, I've also witnessed their worst. Sometimes I even question my own behavior, but I try to trust my heart.

Day 396 — 5 December 1969,
All of the soldiers who came here with me, are no more. "San Fran" my buddy from the West coast befriended a young Vietnamese boy missing several front teeth, that he knick-named, "Smiley." The lad spoke a little broken English and was probably only nine years old, but he has been hanging around the camp for over a week carrying a small wooden box and shining soldier's shoes. Today, San Fran and two other "G.I.'s" were standing in a group when Smiley came into the camp hollering, "Soo Sine, Joe's! Soo Sine!" The trio called the boy over and San Fran propped his boot up on a rock. Smiley knelt in front of them, looked back over his shoulder towards the tree's lining the camp, opened his shoe-shine box and.... ? "KABOOOOOM!" A

deafening explosion resonated through the camp. Smiley, the two soldiers, and my final friend in this awful place were no more.

Day 408 — 17 December 1969,
Death, fear, blood, and horrendous screams make up the nightmare which surrounds me everywhere. Lord, please guide me, lead me... And forgive my weak moments. I wish to serve my country well, but I yearn for home. Although the time of my departure is near, I often have come to believe that it will be in a body bag with a metal tag identifying what is left. I want to forget this awful place, this terrible war,... this Vietnam. The buddies I've lost and why, I ask. I fear at times, my sanity, any decency I ever possessed and even my faith too, I will lose forever. I do however, take heart in a higher cause, a far nobler ideal than I can currently perceive and trust that I have chosen the right path. God, if you are out there still and I must will myself to believe that you most definitely are, for in my heart, I believe it to be true. Please, deliver me safely to the end! If I am meant to join you instead, so be it, but Lord Jesus, please, I beg of you, watch over my dear parents back home.

Ben trembled in his chair, visualizing for a moment, the look of pain that had been in Fred's eyes that Christmas Eve, back in 1972. He now felt even closer to his departed friend than before, because he knew that he himself, hadn't experienced the dark side of humanity alone. Although not at the same time, both he and Fred, had most definitely walked a mile in one another's shoes. Oddly, even after all of these years and while sitting in his recliner in front of the Christmas tree in his own home, Ben became lost in the nightmare that was the war in Vietnam.

He could still hear the rotors of the chopper's pounding the air and the roar of the jets dropping their payloads. He could feel the concussion of mighty blasts, the heat of fiery infernoes against his skin and warm, murky swamp water pouring into his combat boots. Memories of the relentless attack of biting insect along with the itch and stench of "Trench-foot," multiple body rashes, and irritations, made his skin crawl. Even from the chair in his living room now, the memories seem so real that he can hear the yelling, the cursing and the awful screaming.

Echoes of earth-shattering detonations, exploding grenades, machine gun blasts, and the, "Pop!... Pop!... Pop!" of small arms fire resonated through his mind. He could even feel the eerie suspense brought on by the awful silence of the patrols, when you knew that the enemy was close, but where and when would they strike? He knew what it was to lose himself, wonder if he would ever survive and question himself as to if he even really still wanted to survive. He had seen grown men cry like babies, when a "Dear John" letter would crush their only reason for striving onward another day. In Ben's mind, he momentarily returned to the overgrown jungle and could hear the wacking of machetes cutting through the brush. Many were the times when he had heard the sound of knives cautiously sliding from leather sheaths and a fear-instilling and deadly, "WOOOOMPH!" as yet another land-mine went off maiming and annihilating those around him. He had felt the spray of warm blood on his face and heard the impact of flying shrapnel thudding into trees, armament and bodies. Once more Ben could almost feel and smell the burn of an overheated machine gun in his hands. He can sense the fear, the brush of death and almost hear the high pitched whining, "WWWIPPPPFFFH!" of bullets flying by. He momentarily relived the the terrible illnesses, the feverish infections, the adrenaline rushes and the constant fear.

Back came the smells of stale sweat, blood, and damp, rotten vegetation mixed with those of moth balls, gun powder and napalm. He would never forget the rancid odor of the dead, the burning plants, machinery, and human flesh, the filthy camp latrines or the odors emitting from the various means, some soldiers used, to escape that horrid place. As hauntingly real screams of agony pierced through his memories, Ben envisioned himself, once more on patrol. It was a time that he thought he had put behind him, one when each agonizing second of every grueling day, was encompassed with negative outlooks. He had been bombarded with thoughts of extreme terror, fear of never returning home and seeing Sarah ever again, and even the possibility of never being, whom he had once been, ever again. He was proud to be a soldier, but torn between issues of duty and honor. He longed to be proud of his attempts at helping to liberate the people he was there to defend, but the truth was, that he often couldn't tell who was friend or foe, until sometimes it proved to be too late. Also too, came back the feelings of shame he had experienced for doing some of the things he was ordered to do and how the mud and the blood, just would not wash away from his hands.

Ben could see the battle-weary faces of his platoon. Your "Brothers at Arms" and your "Fellow Soldier's," together you were untied by a common bond. Your very lives depended on each other, but like Fred had written, you were afraid to get close and you didn't want to know their names because you knew that many of them were never leave there alive. Ben remembered the numerous times, when no one could hear his emotionally charged cries to God for help, safety, and deliverance. As he sat in his recliner reliving the thirteen dreadful months he had spent in Vietnam he could still hear the raspy voice of his platoon sergeant saying things like, "War, it's glory and chaos rolled up into one. It'll make ya' or break ya', but rest assured that it'll never leave ya'!"

Ben recalled how the propaganda had played with their minds and the haunting stories of torture which would be inflicted, should one become a prisoner of war. He remembered the bodies and even the permanently scarred survivors of those soldiers his outfit discovered, who most unfortunately, had fallen victim to the enemies evil demises. Letters and pictures from home, the occasional care-package which contained items reminding you that a safe, warm, loving, and civilized world still existed out there somewhere beyond the corrupt reality that had become your daily life. That, coupled with fighting to protect the soldier next to you and an intense, yet often wavering faith in God and the belief that you would survive to live yet again in the wonderful world you once did, was often all that kept you surging onward. There were some good times and laughter amidst the turmoil, but oftentimes in people's memories, the good doesn't always outweigh the bad. For many veterans the only good, that ever helped them to rise above the bad they had experienced, developed the day they finally got to go home. That had been true for Ben. He was about ready to put the journal down and take a break because of the memories it was resurrecting, but he decided to read on just a bit further.

Day 413 — 22 December 1969,
Hallelujah! My time in this cursed war is done and it is homeward bound I go! I cannot wait to see, hold and hug Mom and Dad again. It is with bated breath that I eagerly await the opportunity to smell Mom's home-cooking, celebrate Christmas at home and view the star of Christ perched high aloft on the church's Christmas tree. I feared that this debaucherous place had stolen my soul, that I would never experience happiness again, however God has spared me from that most unwanted demise. He has restored my hope and I shall return home from this war with a smile that radiates from within my heart. Never again, shall I harm a living soul. Merry Christmas Jesus! Mom and Dad, your boy, Frederick Flint Stone is returning home!

Reading that last entry caused joy to filter into Ben's heart and a smile broke out upon his face. He could remember how wonderful he felt the day he finally that knew he was going home as well. The good feeling washing over him as he remembered Sarah's smiling face and how wonderful it had felt to feel her in his arms once more, was slightly stifled when he read Fred's next entry, however. Ben's own return had been one of great celebration and he had nearly forgotten that every returning soldier from the Vietnam War hadn't received the same kind of welcome. There were the signs, protests, violent acts and the people whom simply did not understand. Hate had not only existed in Vietnam, Ben sadly acknowledged.

23 December 1969,

I am stateside now, and my heart is full of joy for I shall be home with my parents tomorrow, but I must also admit, that I am somewhat confused. Twelve other fortunate soldiers whom also survived that dreadful war have returned on the same flight as well, so I half expected a celebration when we entered the airport. At the least, perhaps a gracious, "Thank you!" for serving our country. Surely, I was not mistaken for expecting such, but on the contrary, there are people congregated here holding signs that I find rather offensive.

Instead of joyfully shouting, "Welcome home Soldier!" or even offering an early, "Merry Christmas!" the crowd seemed enraged. They even called us aweful names and threw things at us. Their animosity was so overwhelming that I found myself fearing for my safety and rushing across the terminal to escape their mad tirade. Just short of reaching the shelter of the area designated for returning soldiers, a little girl holding her mother's hand, called to me. She was very pretty, all dressed up in the cutest red dress and dainty white shoes with her hair up in ponytails. I paused in my hasty departure to stop, kneel in front of her smiling, and see what it was that she wanted of me. It tore at my heart when shockingly, she glared at me and with great vehemence, hissing, "Die! You… You… Killer!" and she spat upon me.

Why do the people feel this way? I cannot understand. I did my sworn duty, nothing more and nothing less. Yet, I shall not let this most unwelcome of welcomes dampen my spirits. My flight leaves in the morning and I shall spend Christmas Eve in the best of company. I shall rejoice in the Lord! Mom and Dad, I am nearly there!

Ben sat silently for a few moments thinking about the controversies over the Vietnam War and the chaos which had ensued for so many. Then he pictured a young Fred Stone fully decked out in his best "Army Dress," uniform with a duffle bag slung over his shoulder. He envisioned the smile which would have been on his face as he departed that plane on Christmas Eve while he eagerly searched for the welcoming faces of his parents in the terminal. Ben thought once more about how wonderful he himself, had felt upon his own return. He remembered how it felt to once more feel Sarah's heart beating against his chest as he held her tightly, how her perfume smelled and the taste of her lips. He recalled the joy and hugs his family had shared, and as he turned the page in the journal, a smile spread across his face and a warm feeling enveloped his body as he anticipated reading about a warm and joyous welcome for Fred. There was just one entry and the rest of the page was blank. As Ben read it and its words sunk in, his smile slowly disappeared, being replaced with a stunned look of anguish and his very blood ran cold. Ben gasped, "Oh my God!" as he dropped the old ledger into his lap and sagged heavily in his recliner. The dreadful entry staring upward from the time-tarnished page read,

25 December 1969,

Got home yesterday…
Oh God!… Mom?… Dad?… A fire?… Their gone?…
Everything's gone!
I am all alone.
God, how could… ? Why… ?
Now, I know for sure, that you do not love me! So… tell me why?

I have always placed all of my trust in you… but no more…
I'm done with you!"

With his body trembling, Ben slowly looked up and lifted his palms upward in a helplessly futile gesture, silently asking God, "Why?" Now he thought he fully understood the pain and torment he had seen in Fred's eyes beneath that Christmas tree in 1972. Who could fathom what emotional demons and unbearable hardships had besieged him over the three years following that last entry. How did he survive and what led him to the church that night? Ben had no answers, but thinking that perhaps the journal did, he flipped the page and saw that there were more entries. Would they reveal how a devastated man, became the Fred, whom Ben knew?

The mantle-clock bonged in quadruple succession, startling Ben and letting him know that it was 4:00 o'clock. Judging by the dimming light coming through the widow behind the Christmas tree, the sun would soon be down. Realizing he was thirsty, he got up, grabbed a water bottle out of the fridge and checked on Sammi. The little angel was sleeping soundly so Ben quietly returned to the living room with his emotions in a turmoil. Standing in front of the Christmas tree, Ben struggled, trying to make sense out of the often-times, unfair occurrences of life. Grasping his chin with his left hand and shaking his head with confusion, he softly prayed, "It's just not right Lord. I can't help Martha to understand all of this, because it makes no sense at all to me. Fred was too good a man to suffer so much and then... then die the way he did. Where is the fairness in it all?" Ben was torn between wanting to cry and the desire to shake his fists and scream out in anger at Heaven.

He walked over, flopping back into his chair and he began to feel compelled to look at the star atop the Christmas tree. Gazing at it and while wondering why on earth he was doing so, he suddenly heard Fred's deep and gentle voice softly say, "Ben, my friend, you need to read the journal." Oddly, not even questioning the sanity of hearing his deceased friend's voice, he picked up the journal, flipping to the page after the last one he had read minutes ago and resumed reading.

The following entry was one of many that would begin the internal healing process Ben so badly needed. It would lift his sorrowing heart to new heights and help to generate sparks of spiritual understanding, which in turn, would re-ignite his passion for life. The sorrow of having lost a best friend began to be replaced with the joyful memories of having been blessed with such a friend. The Fred, Ben had known and loved came back to life through the words printed before him, beginning with the recording of the first night they met.

24 December 1972,

Lost and Found on Christmas Eve!

As a stranger headed for nowhere, I slowly plodded by;
When the glow of a star within a church, mysteriously caught my eye.
The draw of Christmas beckoned me in;
But I resisted, bound to a vow to never believe or know joy again.

You, O' Lord, knew better and you turned my stubborn head;
It was time to stop living my life, as if I were dead.

Life's left turns had turned me into a most pitiful sight:
But You, O' Lord, wanted to make everything just right.

You guided my feet across the snow, this glorious Christmas Eve;
And safe in your love, I vow never again, to leave.

Oh Lord, please forgive me for the fool I have regretfully been;
Praise, sweet praise I render unto you for taking me back again.

For Ben, Sarah, little Amy, and most certainly, Martha too;
And your dear Son Jesus, I humbly thank You!

Where life will lead me from this night, I do not know;
But I will certainly will be okay, for your love tells me so.

As I lay down my head to rest, I can hear the glorious bells ring;
The angel's chorus of praise to Christ, the Newborn King!

Precious, awe-inspiring, Christmas spirit began to envelop Ben as he read that last verse and he could feel its jubilant fervor coursing through his veins. Joyful memories flooded through his mind as he read through the entries which followed. Some made him laugh and smile and he forgot to be sad for awhile. He remembered the joy of having been Fred's friend and not of how his life had come to an end. The entries were spread over nearly thirty-four years, recording some tough times, but more importantly, the "Good stuff." Picturing each memory as he read, Ben enjoyed them all, but there were those which stood out, head and shoulders above the rest.

25 December 1972,
I thank you Jesus for your goodness to me;
For new friends like Ben, Sarah, and a little angel named Amy.
I thank you for dear Martha, whom has already eternally touched my heart;
Perhaps it may be Thy will, that she and I never part?
Little Amy and I, those sweet candy canes we did share;
And all through the day, your glorious presence was there!"

5 January 1973,
A new job and a brand new start;
Many thanks to a new friend, a gift from the heart.

14 February 1973,
Praise Father, Son and Holy Ghost;
For on this blessed day, I've wed the one I love the most!

23 July 1977,
Endless sweet adoration to you, Oh Lord of mine;
Martha's dreadful tumor, was benign!"

Ben found himself greatly enjoying this stroll down memory lane. He was immensely pleased to see that many of the dates which had been near and dear to Fred's heart, paralleled his own. The two of them truly had been like brothers. Continuing to read through the pages of the journal, Ben stopped here and there, every so often to visualize the events in his mind and relive the roller coaster ride of emotions which had ensued each time.

7 March 1980,
Father, forgive me my doubt, and please restore the hair
I've been losing;
Once again you have answered our prayers, the "Plant" is
not closing!

12 June 1980,
Ben was in an accident today;
Lord, I know that you are good, as I pray!
He broke only his arm and not his head;
When I first saw the car, I feared he was dead.

12 November 1984,
Amy's sixteen and driving today;
Look out everyone, I humorously say.
She's so beautiful as she grows into more of a woman, and
less of a girl;
I thank God for her smile, which lights up the world!

12 June 1993,
To Florida's kingdom of magic, we did go;
The kid in each of us, surely did show!
The rides, the shows, and all the rest;
It's hard to say, what was the best!

30 August 1998,
Amy got married today, but sadly she's moving away;
With her new husband Joe, who promises they will move
back some day.
We're all happy for them, but a little down;
Things just won't be the same, in this old town.

Ben remembered that day well with a bit of humor. He recalled Fred being nearly as upset as he had been, while at the same time they were happy for Amy and Joe. Being grown men, they most certainly couldn't let their wives see tears rolling down their cheeks as the new young couple drove away, now could they? Sarah and Martha did see the tears however, through their own blurred eyes and because of their husband's big hearts, they loved them all the more.

Suddenly, for some reason, Fred had written a list of plants and flowers in the journal, perhaps his plans for a garden and Ben humorously skipped over that section. A page and a half later he found two more wonderful entries recorded, other occasions when the tears had flown, but then they had been tears of joy.

13 January 2001,
Hallelujah! Joe and Amy moved back today;
It is here, that they plan to stay!

9 September 2002,
Against all odds, the doctors did say;
A great miracle occurred today.
After months of emotionally charged prayers;
And casting upon God, all of our cares.
A perfect and precious angel named, Sammi;
Was born to Joe and Amy!
Both mother and baby are doing fine;
So now Sweet Jesus, it's celebration time!

When Amy first announced to the family that she was pregnant, it was a time of great celebration for Ben and Sarah. They were ecstatic about the idea of being grandparents and Fred and Martha were equally excited as well. Although they had no children of their own, they always felt so close to Amy, it was as if she were their daughter too, so they felt like they were going to be grandparents as well. Just like Ben and Sarah, they were dead set on the idea of spoiling the child rotten. They couldn't wait to get started. The course of Amy's pregnancy wasn't just full of eager anticipation however, it also had more than its fair share of anxiety and cause for endless prayers. For the first several months she experienced extreme nausea and was throwing up so much, that her obstetrician began to fear that she might actually begin losing weight. He said that if her condition persisted, she may have to be hospitalized, fed intravenously and re-hydrated. Needless to say, Amy and Joe, Ben, and Sarah, and Fred and Martha worried themselves relentlessly and prayed every chance they got. Then one day, the nausea and the vomiting just stopped cold turkey. Amy started gaining weight and it appeared that everything was going to be okay, until new causes for concern soon surfaced.

At her next doctors appointment they discovered she had anemia. By the following visit, iron supplements had remedied that problem, but then Amy had suddenly developed high blood pressure. She started taking medication, exercised regularly, ate healthier and even managed to squeeze in a cat-nap each afternoon, all at her doctors' direction, but by the 35th week of her pregnancy, the condition had worsened and she was restricted to complete bed rest.

At the beginning of week 37 she started experiencing severe headaches and painful cramping. The doctors ran tests to see what could be wrong, but they found nothing. Then following an ultra-sound, they dropped a bomb shell . They had detected some unknown mass or abnormality in the baby's brain. They were unsure what it was, but they warned the family to be prepared for the worst.

Amy went into labor on the 38th week and Joe went into the delivery room with her. Ben, Sarah, Fred, and Martha sat nervously waiting in the maternity ward's waiting room for six nerve-wracking hours worrying, praying and hoping that both Amy and the baby would be okay.

Ben will never forget that day. It was a Monday, about 5:45 p.m. and the sun was shining through the blinds right into his eyes as he thumbed through the pages of a magazine which he had already looked through three times that afternoon. Sarah and Martha were sitting next to him talking and Fred was standing to one side watching the news on the television hanging from the ceiling. Suddenly the waiting room door burst open and Joe came rushing in. He was beaming from ear to ear, and announced that Amy had just given birth to a beautiful baby girl and that both baby and mother were doing just great.

Ben relived all of this from his recliner in just mere seconds, but the image that lingered for a moment or two in his recollections was a scene from later in that wonderful day. He and Fred were standing outside the observation window of the hospital's nursery looking at the little newborn angel whom now held the key to both of their hearts. Little Samantha Marie Welsh, as her parents named her, lay in a crib just on the other side of the glass. Her beautiful, sparkling eyes looked about as if she were checking out the world. Ben was bubbling with love and joy inside and he could still feel that same emotion now, but for some unexplainable reason, Fred's presence that day, now seemed to be more significant. Ben remembered looking over at Fred and seeing tears of joy in his eyes as he looked down at the newest addition to the family. His eyes were fixed on her precious little face and something happened that Ben had never really given any serious thought about, until now.

Samantha's eyes stopped moving about and stared straight into Fred's eyes as if she were looking into his very soul. He glanced at Ben with a huge smile and then turning back to her, he softly spoke. Thinking about that day now, Ben could almost hear his friends baritone voice gently utter, "Ah's gonna call ya' Sammi, L'il Darlin', an' ah'll make ya, dis' promise. Ole' Fred'll make sho' ya' stays safe an' thet' nuttin' bad e'er happens ta' ya'!'"

Ben could sure relate to that sentiment, for there was then, and never will be, a single thing he wouldn't do to protect his precious princess. Instead of calling her Samantha, however Ben took such a liking to Fred's knick-name for her, that he and nearly everyone else have called her Sammi, ever since.

People often say that babies can't see very far and that they probably don't think like we do. They say they can't possibly understand us when we talk to them and that if they smile, it's gas. Ben will forever argue those opinions, because somehow just now, while remembering that day, he has realized that Fred made a promise to little Sammi through that nursery window and it was one that she somehow understood. She had even smiled at him and it wasn't a case of "Gas." Ben scratched his head, feeling a bit puzzled, as if God were trying to tell him something important with that acknowledgement, but it made no sense. He looked upward in wonder for a second thinking, "God, Fred's gone and so is his promise. How is knowing this going to help anyone now?" Slowly shaking his head and deciding there's no use in trying to figure it out now, Ben decided to continue reading the journal. The next several entries brought back more good memories..

22 September 2002,
A great event, took place today;
I'm so happy, that all I can say!
Is to God, be all glory and praise;
Little Sammi was baptized today!

11 December 2002,
Ben and I, finished Sammi's room;
Much to our wives' delight.
It's a perfect princess bedroom;
For when she comes to spend the night!

14 February 2003,
Thirty blessed marital years, together we have spent;
My beautiful, precious Martha and I.
I thank you Lord, for this angel you have sent;
And all our years together as time passes quickly by!

27 April 2003,
The towns 150th birthday has come and gone, I'm quite
relieved to say;
For now, I can finally shave this itchy beard away.

Reading that last entry left Ben smiling with relief as he rubbed his chin and remembered the joy of having to itch no more. He, Fred, and nearly every other man in town had grown beards to commemorate the event, and why? Because way back in 1853, just six months after the naming of the town had become official, a certain political "Abe" stopped in town on his way to Illinois. The funny thing was that with his beard, Fred resembled a shorter version of the tall lanky rail-splitter, so much so, that at the plant and all about town, everyone referred to him as "Honest Stone." The name hung with him for a long time, even after he shaved off the beard. Ben sat smiling as he pictured his skinny friend with his profound adams-apple and beard. Each time Fred heard someone make a presidential reference towards him, he'd saunter over next to them, pull out a five dollar bill and wave it in front of them. When they instinctively tried to grab it, he'd snatch it back, stick out his chest, strike a dignified pose and in a mock, deeply distinctive voice he would drawl, "Ah' sho' hopes ya'll liked muh pictia'."

Ben paused in his reminiscing to look at the clock and it was a quarter past the hour. He thumbed through the remaining pages of the journal and seeing that he was nearly finished with it, he gave into the compelling urge to read until the end. He reasoned with himself that it could do no harm to let Sammi nap for just ten more minutes. Besides, reading the journal so far was working like a miracle drug, diminishing the sorrow which has assailed him ever since Fred died, and Ben desperately needed the healing. The next several entries brought back more of the good memories causing Ben to experience internal feelings of happiness, such as he had thought, he may never feel again.

17 September 2003,
I scratched a lottery ticket once again;
And this time a substantial prize, I did win.
Yes, it is gambling I must confess;
But, it sure felt good, none the less.

9 September 2005,
Today Amy's precious angel turned three;
And like so many others, Sammi found cause to laugh at me.
She discovered the meaning of the, "F" in Frederick F. Stone;
And my yabba dabba secret was suddenly known.

25 December 2005,
Today was the best Christmas ever;
A day I will forever treasure.
At Ben's, to Sammi, a story I told,
One she will remember, even when she grows old;
The story of the candy cane you see;
And how it signifies, that we are indeed, free!

Ben remembered the story clearly, for when Fred had told it, he too had been listening along with everyone else that day. They were all gathered around the Christmas tree in the living room and Ben, with Sammi perched on his lap, sat right where he was seated now. The presents had been opened, they had feasted like royalty, and now, warm conversation filled the air. From out of who knows where, Sammi suddenly produced a half eaten candy cane, most likely the remains of the one she had received from church the night before.

"Gimmie a bite!" Ben teased and Sammi jumped off of his lap and onto her feet, preparing to dart away full of smiles and giggles. She dropped the candy cane onto the coffee table next to his recliner and ran to hide behind Fred who was standing near the tree talking to Ben's father. "Save me Fwed!... Save me, pweeze!" she shrieked with delight as Ben taunted her from his recliner. Fred turned and knelt down in front of Sammi and said in his deep voice, "It'll cost ya' a big hug!" Sammi threw her arms around him, more than happy to render payment. Soon, the two of them were carrying on like there's no tomorrow, oblivious to the rest of the room. Ben had to holler, "Sammi!" three times before he was able to get her attention and then feigning a look of hurt and neglect he sadly whined, "Hey, come back here. Where's my hug? Don't you love me no more?"

Sammi came barreling across the floor and dove back up into his lap as she hollered, "Wight' here I am, PamPaw!... I wuv' you!" and she threw her little arms around his and kissed his cheek. Ben began tickling Sammi who giggled and squirmed and pretty soon she was begging for him to tell her a story. He told her one story about Christmas, but she wanted more. He told her another about outer space, and yet she wasn't satisfied. After a third story, this one about a little girl and her pony, Ben was out of ideas. Sammi impatiently started demanding, "mo' stowies!... Mo' stowies PamPaw!" As she bounced up and down in Ben's lap chanting, "Mo!... Mo!... Mo!" Fred walked up next to the recliner, looking like he was on the verge of saying something.

He picked up the remains of Sammi's candy cane and looked at it for a moment before sitting next to them in Sarah's recliner. Losing his drawl and sounding much like a fancy butler in a ritzy mansion he said, "I beg your pardon Ms. Welsh, but perhaps I may interest you in a story? You may find it pleasing, were I to share the story of the candy cane with you?" Sammi's eyes opened wide as she shook her head up and down, laughed and said, "You funny, Fwed!" Fred resumed his usual country banter stating, "Ah' sho' am L'il Darlin! Ah' sho' am!" He looked around the room smiling and holding up the candy cane for everyone to see, he began to tell his story.

"Dis' here story, ah's bout' ta' tell all' y'all happened back a fer' piece. Ya see, der' was dis' fella, a candy maker, thet' lived in Indiana. He done went, n' decided he wanted ta' make a special candy fer' Christmas, one thet' would remind pert near everybody of da' real reason fer' da' season. He ciphered long and hard b'fer he cum up with what he done reckin'd was the rawt' qualities fer' da' candy. First off he made his self a stick of hard, pure white candy. Ya'all see, da white stood fer' da' virgin birth of da' Lord's one an' only perfect n' sinless Son, Jesus. Dat' hardness to da' candy rep-a-sented him a be'in' da' churches one solid foundation and da fact thet' God's promises are fer' real."

Fred paused looking around the room, his eyes coming to rest on Sammi sitting fully attentive in Ben's lap. Her eyes were wide with wonder and Fred resisted the urge to lean over and give her a big hug. Once again, he held up the candy cane for the whole room to see and after clearing his throat, he resumed telling his story.

"Y'all see dis here shape of da' candy? Some people say it's shaped like a 'J' ta' stand fer' Jesus. Other's say it peers ta' be more like a shepherd's staff, da Good Shepherd's staff that is. When we see's it, we kin' think bout' how Jesus reaches down from Heav'n, an' reclaims us, whin' like fallen lambs, we hev' done went an' gone astray. These here red stripes, why dey' stands fer' da' blood thet' Christ done went an' shed fer' us all. Lastly, dat sweet n' minty taste let's us know thet' God's love is good n' refreshin'. So, now y'all knows the story of da' candy cane."

When Fred finished speaking, he handed the half eaten candy cane back to Sammi. It was apparent that she had listened really well, for she immediately turned to face Ben, pointed at the candy and said, "Wook PamPaw. White mean Baby Jesus. Wed' is his bwood'. 'J' is fo Jesus sheppod's staff." Then she smiled, popped the candy cane into her mouth and exclaimed,

"PamPaw, Jesus is goooooood!" Everyone laughed hysterically as Fred said, "Yes siree Sammi, He sho' is!"

Looking up from his chair and over at the clock, Ben realizes that he needs to awaken Sammi in a few minutes to run her home, but there is just one entry left in the journal. He feels a strong, yet strange urging to read it now as well. Looking down, he realizes that this entry is somehow different. Never once during reading the rest, had he found it odd that Fred so often, had written in verse. Rather, he found that it spoke very well, for the man he had called his best friend . This last entry is not in verse however, or even in a cultured over-tone. An eerie sensation settles over Ben causing him to feel like he is about to unveil a past premonition of sorts. The entry is written more like Fred usually tended to talk and as Ben reads it, he can hear his deceased friend's giant-like voice once more.

28 September 2006,
"Well, today ah' retired from da' Plant, after pert near thirty-fo' years. Ah' sho' do thank Ben fer' gittin' me thet job fer it's been a good un'. Now Martha and I will hev' time ta' do all da' things we've always wanted to,... maybe? In da' mawnin' Ben n' I are fixin' ta' go a fishin', but I jest' don't know. Somethin's been eatin' at me lately an' it scares me a bit. Ah' feel good and happy most of the time, but I bin' gittin' the feelin' thet' I'm a headin' ta' Heav'n' soon. Ah' worry fer' Martha, but if'n God says it's time, then' I reckin I hev' ta' be ready. Years ago, on thet' one extra special Christmas Eve, I were bout' as fer' from bein ready ta' meet God as a fella' kin' git', but da' Lord, Jesus Christ, done brought me round.
"God, ah' knows thet' if'n ya'll calls me homeward, ah'll be missed by Martha, Ben, Sarah and da' family. L'il Sammi, bless her heart, she'll miss me too. Ah' want ta' keep muh' promise ta' her, da' one ta' keep her safe, but if'n Ya'll calls me away, ah' know's ya' will do da' job fer' me. Thinkin' bout' goin' away makes muh' sad, till ah'

remember. We'll all gather together agin' in Heav'n one day, and we'll hev' one big shin-dig. Jesus, ah' must apologize fer once ah' thought ya hated me, but now I know thet' ya love me. If'n I come home sooner, rather than later, please hep' Martha ta' make it through. Let both her n' Ben, each know, thet' ah'm at peace with muh'self n' happy in Heav'n with All Ya'll. "Hep dem' ta' know thet' ah' loved em' an' would hev' liked mo' time with em', but you had something' bigger planned fer' me an' thet's okay. Life will go on an' it'll be fine fer dem' ta' be happy agin."

Time, ah' now realize like sands runnin' thru an hourglass, waits fer' no one. Pert ne'er ever-thin' is cordin' ta' God's plan, n' it's not always fer' us ta' knows da' when, how, where n' why of things. It ain't at all, bout' bein' fair. It's bout' livin, not jest now, but fo'eva'. All any of us kin do is ta' hang on tight to da' one thing thet'll keep us a headin' in da' rawt' direction,... Hope! Sometimes da' journey'll be tough, but if'n we let him, Jesus will gladly lead da' way. Ah' believe thet' da' destination is well worth experiencin' da' ride. Mom and Dad, ah've sho' missed ya, but roll out the welcome mat, cause I may be a comin' home soon!"

Ben wiped tears away from his eyes as he closed the journal feeling like a great load had been lifted off of his shoulders. He still missed Fred, and didn't understand why he had to die, but now the happiness they had shared through the years, by far, outweighed the sadness he'd been lugging around with him ever since that September day. He stood up stretching his stiffened back, arms and legs. They were complaining, letting him know that he wasn't as young as he used to be. His snow-removal escapades of the day were going to cost him dearly. The clock on the mantle said it was almost 4:30 p.m. and time to wake up Sammi. Ten minutes later they were both back in Ben's truck, singing Christmas carols with the radio once more, and headed towards Sammi's house.

On the way out of the door, on impulse he had quickly grabbed Fred's journal and the envelope bearing Martha's name on it, knowing that it would be the perfect Christmas present for her, and stuck it down in his coat's side pocket. He had placed his own letter from Fred inside the Bible sitting on his desk in the study. He wasn't sure of when or where he was going to present the journal to Martha, but he did know that she needed it. Ben hoped that it helped her as much as it had him. It's effect on him was nothing short of stupendous, for despite his body's protesting the days events, he was feeling so good inside that he was tempted to try and kick his heels together. He abstained from the urge however, for no proud grandpa wants to fall flat on his rump right in front of his favorite four year old admirer.

There's one thing Ben would have to admit. Christmas Eve was certainly turning out a whole lot better than it had started.

CHAPTER FOURTEEN

It was almost dark, but the town was bustling with activity. The Christmas decorations on the light poles were beginning to light up as were the decorations adorning nearly every yard and business in the town. The traffic was heavy and shoppers were hurrying in and out of the stores anxiously making their last minute purchases. One block from Sammi's house, in the glow cast by a lighted, plastic nativity set displayed in front of a brick ranch, three kids were having a snowball fight . One of them was hiding behind a huge snowman with a giant red Christmas bow hanging on his chest like a tie. "Wook PamPaw! Snowman!" Sammi exclaimed as she pointed. When they pulled into the drive at her house, a rabbit took off, out from under a bush and across the snow covered yard. "Hi, MamMaw!" Sammi yelled as she scooted past Sarah, who met them at the front door and greeted Ben with a kiss.

The aroma of fresh-baked cookies made Ben realize that he was hungry again as he went in the house. Sammi, was all excited as she told her mother, grandmother and Martha all about her day with Ben while he just stood back beaming as any proud grandfather would.

After a few minutes Sammi's excited banter became directed at her mother and Ben asked Sarah and Martha if they were ready to go. They both realized, that ready or not, they had better get going, because there was still quite a bit of stuff needing to be done before going to church later. While Martha was putting on her coat and getting her things together, Sarah came over to Ben smiling kind of peculiarly and she gave him a great big hug. "What's that for?" he asked, a little curious. "Because it's Christmas Eve and I love you, and..." she leaned close so Martha wouldn't hear her and whispered, "And because, for the first time since Fred died, you finally look as though you're feeling okay."

Ben was surprised for he did indeed feel a million times better than he had and he asked, "I am okay now, but how did you know, Honey?" Sarah smiled and replied, "Because I can see a glow in your eyes that I haven't seen for quite a while, and I'll bet it has something to do with that, doesn't it?" She pointed down at Ben's coat pocket where the old, worn and soiled edge of a book could be seen sticking up. "It's Fred's journal, isn't it," Sarah asked quietly. Ben was shocked as he replied, "Yeah, actually it is, but how could you have known about it? I never even knew that he kept one." Sarah leaned back, looking up into Ben's eyes and gently poking him in the ribs she teased, "So you're admitting you don't know everything, huh?" After waiting a few seconds for the implication to sink in she added, "Martha told me that he kept one and that she has been anxiously searching for it ever since,... well you know when. The poor Dear, she's been having such an awful time and she misses him so very much. She's been hoping to find the journal and possibly find some words of comfort in it, anything to help her to quit crying every night. Where on earth did you find it?" Ben looked at her and softly answered, "It fell out of my truck's glove compartment today when I was getting Sammi out of her car seat. It caught me by complete surprise, but you know, reading it has seemed to lift the cloud of sorrow thats been hanging over me ever since the accident. I can't even explain it, but when I was going through the journal, I felt like Fred was there with me, telling me that everything is okay. Sarah, I wish I would have found it weeks ago and I wonder, how come I didn't know about the journal before today?"

Sarah just smiled with still yet another version of, "The look" this one being the "All-knowing look" as she suggested, "Maybe because you weren't supposed to know before today. God has his reasons." Ben just shook his head and said, "I guess he does. Fred must have put the journal in my glove box the day of the accident, and do you want to hear something really weird? There were two letters in it, one for me and the other for Martha." Now it was Sarah's turn to be surprised as she looked at Ben with widened eyes and asked, "A letter to you? What did it say?"

Suddenly Martha walked up saying, "What did what say?" Ben just replied, "Oh, it's nothing Martha. Are you ready to go?" He hugged and kissed Sarah, whispering, "I'll tell you more about it later," and then he said aloud, "I'll see you at home, Honey." He walked over to the kitchen counter where Amy and Sammi were eating cookies and talking about the snow angels Sammi had made. Ben attempted to distract them with a group hug as he swiped two cookies for himself, but Sammi caught him and squealed, "PamPaw took cookies Mommy!" Ben feigned surprise saying, "What?... Who me?" He gave Sammi one of the cookies and stuck the other one entirely in his mouth and held up his hands as if to say, "What cookies?" Amy just shook her head at him as Sammi tried to imitate him with the cookie he had given her.

Ben kissed his keen-eyed little princess on the forehead, winked at Amy and said, "I'll see you girls at church after while." As he prepared to follow Martha out the door, Sarah walked up, wiped a smudge of chocolate from the corner of his mouth and said, "Hey, Cookie Bandit, I have one last stop to make and I'll be home soon."

It was starting to spit a little snow again as Ben and Martha walked out to his truck and although it was dark now, the snow made the world bright enough that you could still easily see. On the way to Martha's house, they carried on in idle chit-chat about Christmas, the snow and Sammi's latest antics. Although Fred's name didn't come up in their conversation, he knew that she was thinking about him and missing him more than ever.

Ben urgently wanted to tell Martha about the journal, but he was a bit apprehensive, because he didn't want to possibly upset her on Christmas Eve. He resisted the urge to just blurt out his afternoon discovery, but he wanted to help her to feel better, like he did now.

As they pulled into Martha's driveway Ben glanced over at her and he could detect the pain hidden just below the surface of her forced-happy demeanor and he wished that he could make it go away. Fred had written in his letter, that Ben would know the right time to present the journal to Martha, and almost as if on cue, when he shut off the truck and switched off the headlights, something told his heart that the moment had arrived. As Martha gathered her things, he asked her, "Martha, are you really doing okay?"

He recognized the fake smile she instantly put on, for it greatly resembled the same false expression he had been wearing himself a lot lately. Martha sighed and replied, "Oh Ben, it's hard, but I'm doing okay." She turned towards the window and in the glow cast into the cab by her yard light, Ben could see the sparkle of a tear in the corner of her eye as she whispered, "I just miss him so much." She turned back to Ben, wiping away the tear, smiled wryly and changing the subject she said, "I can't wait to see Sammi in her angel costume tonight." Ben's heart hurt for Martha as he replied, "Me neither!" Reaching down and grasping the edge of the old book in his coat pocket and said, "Well Martha, I guess we'll be over to pick you up for church about twenty minutes before seven o'clock, but before I go, I want to give you a something special. I believe it's the one thing that will make you feel a hundred percent better, and you could even say that it's a Christmas present,... from Fred. I just found it today," and then he handed her the journal with the envelope bearing her name, tucked inside.

Martha's eyes widened and instantly filled with tears as she put her hand to her cheek and gasped, "Oh my Lord!" With shaking hands, she took the journal and stared at it completely speechless for a moment. Ben reached out and put his hand on her shoulder squeezing gently and said, "Read it Martha. I promise, it will help." She nodded as more tears filled her eyes and she clutched the journal tightly to her chest and looked up towards heaven. Her lips were moving and although no audible sounds could be heard, Ben knew that she was thanking the Lord for Fred's gift.

As he helped Martha to the front door of her house he could feel her anxious, yet hesitantly nervous desire to read words Fred had left behind. As she went into her house she thanked Ben for the ride and the journal. He turned towards his truck and replied, "You're quite welcome Martha. We'll see you after while, okay?" He heard her sniffle as she closed the door and his heart ached for her. He earnestly hoped that the journal would help her like it had him. Reading it would cause her to relive memories, just as it had Ben, but would those memories in turn, bring on happiness from the joy they had shared together, or a renewed onslaught of pain from the tragedy of sudden loss and knowing that no new memories were going to be created with her soul-mate, not at least on this side of forever?

Two minutes later the truck was parked in his own shed and Ben was plugging in two extension cords which led to the alternating red and green strings of Christmas lights hung in the bushes in front of his house. His thoughts were now ranging from concern for Martha, to tantalizing visions of the home-made chili cooking in the crock pot inside. As he walked towards the house he could faintly smell it in the air and his stomach grumbled in hungry appreciation. The sound of partly melted and refrozen snow crunching under his feet echoed across the yard. A cold wind came from out of nowhere, sending a chill up Ben's spine, causing him to pull his coat a little tighter. "The snow is sure pretty, but I can do without the cold." Ben thought to himself.

Then suddenly, somewhere in the darkness a cardinal's whistle echoed across his yard and it drew Ben's attention feeling like a moment of "déjà vu." He paused looking into the star lit sky and noticed the blinking light of a passenger jet which was more than likely filled with excited passengers flying home for the holiday. It had started to snow lightly and Ben could feel the fresh, cold, snowflakes fall softly against his cheeks as he curiously wondered about the cardinal's greeting. Again, the crimson caroler's call sounded forth and Ben remembered a night, exactly two years ago when he and Fred had just returned from getting some last minute Christmas gifts in town, after work, for their wives. It was a Friday night had been unseasonably warm with the threat of rain in the air. Then too, just as tonight, Ben had parked in the shed and was plugging in the Christmas lights. Fred was heading across the yard to his house, when a similar cardinal's call echoed through the night. As Ben stepped out of the shed Fred's deep voice boomed from the dark shadows of the yard, "Lis'n ta' thet' will ya Ben? Mista' Red's a sayin', 'Merry Christmas ya'll and good night!' Do ya' hear it?" Tonight, the cardinal whistled a third time and from across the snow-covered landscape, Ben swore he heard Fred's voice once more utter, the exact same words in echo to its refrain.

Ben began to feel warm all over and he realized that he now knew without a doubt, that even though Fred had died, he wasn't really gone. The memories of the joy experienced with him are still here and Martha, Ben and his family will see him again some day. The pains of loss and sorrow will still hurt immensely and more tears will most definitely fall, but it's okay to let happiness back into life. When seemingly unfair circumstances kick us in the teeth, and we lose all desire to move forward, God still wants to lift us up. Everything is truly going to be alright, even if there are those countless numbers of times when our faith falters, circumstances slap us in the face and every logical sense of reasoning seems to scream, "Nothing will ever be okay again!" The answers we so desperately seek for, as to the "Why?" of life's seeming unfairness may continue to elude us, but in the grand scheme of things, rest assured, the good in life will always triumph over the bad.

Ben strongly believed all of this and more, as he bid farewell to the mysterious cardinal in the hidden dark shadows of the yard, and he was whistling when he went into the house.

CHAPTER FIFTEEN

Headlights flashed through the living room window and flickered throughout the house instantly followed by the vibrating sound of the garage door opening. Ben smiled, knowing that Sarah was home. A glance at the microwave clock told him that it was 5:35 p.m. and he had just finished setting the table. "Perfect timing," he uttered aloud as he glanced over his handiwork, and smoothed out a wrinkle in the red tablecloth he had found stowed away in one of the kitchen drawers. He switched on a small fiber optic Christmas tree which he had placed on the table as a center piece and double checked the sprig of mistletoe he had hung from the chandelier over the table. Then he quickly darted over to the wall, dimmed the light and positioned himself to one side of the table as "I'll Be Home for Christmas," started playing from the kitchen radio. He anxiously watched the door that led to the garage, eager to see the look on Sarah's face when she came into the room. Call it weird if you want, but even at the age of sixty-six and after forty-three years of marriage, Ben still felt it important to try to impress Sarah every once in a while and tonight was one of those times. He realizes that he has been an emotional anchor as of late, and it's high time that he gets back to being the, 'Ben Chambers' everyone knows.

He inadvertently held his breath as the door opened and Sarah came into the kitchen carrying two bags and her purse saying, "Honey, I'm home! Mmmm, Mmmmm! It sure does smell good in here." She put her things on the counter and seeing Ben standing in the shadows of the adjoining dining room, she headed his way, checking out the table. After glancing up at the mistletoe, a big smile broke out across her face. "Merry Christmas Darling," Ben exclaimed.

Sarah's beautiful gaze of approval accompanied by the passionate hug and long, gentle kiss which followed, was just the reward Ben had been hoping for. His attempt at holiday romance was nothing big or fancy, but after all, it's the thought that counts, right? He took on the air of a dignified head waiter at a five-star restaurant as he seated his "Better Half," and placed her napkin in her lap. She noticed with a glance of admiration, that Ben had gotten out some of the good china, silverware and crystal wine glasses for their dinner, but that's about where the elegance stopped.

The only formal attire Ben owned was a black suit that he wore to weddings, funerals and important events, so the waiter whom seated Sarah this evening simply sported blue jeans, a flannel shirt, her favorite aftershave and socked feet. She found him irresistible none the less. The napkin he placed in her lap was a flower printed paper towel and sweetened iced tea filled the long stemmed glasses which sparkled in the changing colorful glow cast by the little fiber optic tree. Each place setting was composed of a plate bearing several slices of cheese, a bowl and a soup spoon. Off to one side of Sarah's plate stood a decorative cracker tin.

Ben carefully carried the steaming crock pot full of delicious smelling chili in from the kitchen and after setting it on a hot pad on the table he produced a ladle from his back pocket and filled their bowls. As Ben took his seat, Sarah leaned forward, taking a deep breath and savored the aroma of her great grand-mother's renowned chili recipe. Her stomach growled, letting its hunger be known and Ben had to poke a little fun at her suggesting that she release the ravenous beast lurking inside her. Then he leaned over, pointed up to the mistletoe and kissed her again before they bowed their heads to pray.

As their, 'Amen's' echoed in unison, her stomach rumbled again and Ben just stared at her with a wry smile that led her to think that he was searching for a wisecrack. His seemingly mischievous eyes followed her as she reached for the cracker tin. When she took off the lid and started to reach inside, Ben took a breath and she wondered what animal he was going to compare her internal grumblings to this time. She was searching her mind for a witty come-back, when suddenly, instead of grabbing crackers inside the tin, her fingers closed on a small black velvet box with a red ribbon wrapped around it. "Surprise! Merry Christmas Darling!" Ben shot out with a big smile as curiosity filled her mind and she withdrew the ingeniously hidden secret gift.

"Oh Ben, what did you do?" Sarah asked as her faced flushed scarlet. Ben thought that she looked like an angel in the glow of the fiber optic tree as he said, "It's just a little early Christmas present, Dear. Open it up." She carefully slipped the ribbon from the box, lifted the lid and peered inside. There, on a pad of cotton, lay a beautiful diamond necklace sparkling like raindrops in the sunlight and it looked awful familiar. Sarah suddenly realized with a gasp, that it was the very necklace that she and Martha had discovered while wish-shopping in, "Harmstead's Jewelry Store" back in September. It looked just like a necklace her grandmother had given her the day she and Ben were married, one that sadly had been stolen, many years ago.

Sarah had planned to tell Ben about the necklace and hint around that perhaps it would make a good Christmas present, but before she could, Fred's accident had occurred and she had since forgotten about it. "Oh Ben... It's beautiful... and just like... ?" Ben finished her statement for her saying, "Just like the one your grandmother gave you, right?" Surprise showed in Sarah's eyes as she stammered, "Y... yes, but how did you know? I never told you about it." At first Ben just smirked slyly and replied, "Oh, I have my ways," but after a few seconds he added, "Actually, the thanks goes to Fred."

Ben hesitated for a few seconds, enjoying the look of confusion that wrinkled Sarah's forehead before he added, "Martha told Fred that you found it down at "Harmstead's." He told me about it, so I snuck down and bought it just a few days before Fred... (sharp pain struck momentarily at Ben's heart, but he forced it aside as he concluded)... was killed." A short moment later, Sarah got out of her chair and threw her arms around Ben, thanking and kissing him which made it pretty easy for him to feel good inside, despite the pain of missing Fred lurking in the shadows of his subconscious once more. "I've got an early present for you too!," Sarah said with excitement in her voice. She wheeled around, walked over to the kitchen counter and grabbed one of the two bags she had brought in. "I'm sorry that it's not wrapped, but I want you to have it now" she said as she handed him the bag and sat back down in her seat while searching his face for his reaction. Now it was Ben's turn to be curious as he reached into the bag to discover what was hidden inside.

Surprise and joy, plus a small pulsating sense of sorrow settled over Ben as his attention focused on Sarah's gift. It was a 8" X 10" photograph mounted in a stylized "North Woods" frame which had, "Precious Memories" scrolled into its design. The picture instantly put a smile on his face, but also threatened to fill Ben's eyes with tears. It made him smile and sigh with laughter, yet at the same time, it reopened a painful void deep within his heart. For a few tense moments, he was completely speechless as he sat staring at the image and Sarah watched his eyes, curious to see if he liked it or not. Ben's mind traveled back, nearly three months ago, to a moment he'd completely forgotten about, until now. It was early in the evening, on the 28th of September, the night before the awful tragedy which took Ben's best friend away.

You could say that it was, "The calm before the storm," for it had been a wonderful time, full of fun and excitement as they prepared to celebrate Fred's official retirement. Ben would never have imagined, not even in a million years, that such exhilarating joy so quickly could turn into one of the most devastating periods of his life. "God, it's not fair," he silently thought once more, but this time the heated passion in that statement wasn't as intense as it had been before. He stared down at the faces in the picture, unaware that Sarah had reached over and put her hand on his arm. She had struggled with the thought of giving Ben this particular gift, hoping that it would bring him happiness, yet scared that it would possibly cause him more suffering in his grief. After seeing the change in him earlier, after his discovery of Fred's journal, Sarah felt that perhaps the gift would be like, "Icing on the cake." Now, full of great concern, she silently sat watching his face, noticing the moisture in his eyes and trying to read what was going through his mind as he stared at the framed reminder of a happy time. She silently wondered, "Did I make a big mistake?"

The picture was of Little Sammi, Fred and Ben clowning around in their new john boat as it sat in its trailer parked on the shed drive. All of them had been so excited about celebrating Fred's official retirement, that Sarah just had to take pictures. She had forgotten about taking them that night, until a week ago. She was looking in a store, trying to get Christmas present ideas for Ben, when she found the picture frame and for some unknown reason, it caused a stir of excitement to course through her. She instantly remembered taking the pictures the night before the accident and after purchasing the frame she rushed home to remove the memory card from her digital camera and review its photos on the computer. There were around twenty pictures in all, but two of them seemed to jump off at the screen at her as if shouting, "Pick us!"

One was a comical picture of Fred and Martha, which Sarah knew she had to frame and give to her own best friend. Fred had tried his best to get Martha to stand in the boat with him for the picture, but after receiving a look of, "Are you nuts?" from her, he conceded to standing beside the boat, but he still insisted on an action shot saying with a slow deep drawl, "Jest a standin' thar an sayin' cheese, is plumb borin' Darlin', Ya' see." Although she was reluctant at first, he got her to put on a life jacket and a fishing hat covered with lures. It went really well with her black Capri's and lilac blouse. Fred had placed a fishing rod in her hands and run the string out and tied it to a tree branch outside the view of the picture. He then put on a bright orange life-vest, dangled a fish scale from his right side belt loop and stood behind Martha. He wrapped his arms around her, grasping her hands and together, they arched the fishing rod back, giving off the appearance of pulling in a monstrous fish from the deep seas.

Dangling over their heads was a red, white, and yellow bobber compliments of Ben who held the rod and reel the floating orb was attached to. It really didn't matter that you could see grass and pavement under their feet, because by the time Sarah snapped the picture, Fred had Martha laughing hysterically and the image was priceless. Sarah had found a frame which suited Martha well and she planned to give it to her later tonight after church, hoping that it too, would be received with joy and elicit no sorrow.

The photograph Sarah selected for Ben was of a comical nature as well, once again being Fred's ingenious idea. Ben was sitting at one end of the boat, arching back on a fishing pole, whose line was tied to an oarlock hidden behind Sammi. She appeared simply adorable with her dark curls sticking out beneath the fishing lure hat, wearing a bright yellow sundress with a lime green life-vest. She was standing in the middle of the boat with one leg kicked back, leaning away from her grandpa and towards Fred who was in turn, leaning towards her with a big fishing net poised as if to scoop her up in it. The smiles on each of their faces in the picture reflected the fun they having. It was just one of those special times, the ones that good memories are made from. Tonight as Ben sat staring into the photgraph, he suddenly recalled hearing Fred tease Sammi in his unforget-table voice, "Ya' got a big un' Ben! Reel er' in!" and he felt that joy once more. Sarah was greatly relieved as she saw Ben's grim features develop into a huge smile and he looked at her with a genuine glow of happiness in his eyes.

"Do you like it?" she asked him, already knowing that he did indeed. Ben took her hand, saying, "It's perfect and I love it! Thank you!" He kissed her and then they spent the next twenty minutes enjoying the chili, while talking about their day's events, Ben's discovery of Fred's journal and how it had helped him. They both hoped that it will do the same for Martha. By the end of supper, they were feeling refreshed and looking forward to seeing Sammi's angel performance in the Children's Christmas Eve program at the church. By 6:15 p.m., they had the kitchen and dining room cleaned up and were busy getting themselves ready for an evening of Yuletide celebration. The poinsettia, which Sarah had found and loved, was now sitting on she and Ben's bedroom dresser. The sounds of a shower running and the whirring of Ben's electric razor drifted down the hallway of the house.

Out in front of the house, barely visible in the glow of the Christmas lights, a hungry racoon is devouring kernels of corn that have fallen from Ben's feeders. The temperature has dropped just a bit more from where it was an hour ago and although the falling snowflakes have increased in size, they pose no threat to the evening's holiday travel. An occasional breeze stirs up a swirl of snow and somewhere in the distance, a dog is barking. Across the street, the Rodgers' boys are hooting and hollering, all abound with Christmas excitement as their parents try to get them to come inside and get ready for their own evenings celebration. A snowplow rumbles by on the road out front, spreading salt in its wake, followed by several impatient drivers, all whom are anxious to get where they were going.

All across the snowy landscape, colorful decorations light up the night and the magic of the season fills the imagination of both young and old. The joy of a Savior's birth and the anticipation of gifts, good food and fellowship with friends and loved ones only adds to the miracle that is Christmas. Inside the Chambers' home, Sarah is putting on her make-up and Ben is shaving away a five o'clock shadow as he hums an old Advent hymn. The good tidings and great memories which will derive from this night are only just beginning, but the masked marauder dining in front of the house, gives all of this, no thought. His only concern is filling his belly and he pauses, but a moment, when a hoot owl's distant and mysterious call reminds him of the dangers of the night.

Experience has taught him well and he is a survivor. Throughout his short life he has seen members of his brood fall victim to the hazards of both nature and man, yet he himself, remains unscathed. He has known extreme hunger and complete fulfillment. On occasion, he has been too hot, too cold and often, just right. He has experienced his fair share of both sickness and health. Death may claim him early or when he is old, and although he does exercise caution, he spends no time worrying about the unknown. Right now, he doesn't even look up at the pick up truck with a lighted Christmas tree in the bed, going by on the road and its less than a hundred and fifty feet away. He just continues to indulge upon the corn he has found finding contentment in the small things. He lives each day to its fullest, for whether he is here or when he's gone, life will still, as it inevitably always does, continue to go on.

CHAPTER SIXTEEN

The very second that Sarah laid eyes on her mother "Helen", when she and Ben picked her up at the assisted living center where she resided, the chattering started. Ben was slightly amused as he listened to them, wondering how they found time to breath. He was heading back towards home, not to pick up a forgotten item, but to actually pick up Martha next door. As he pulled into Martha's driveway, Sarah suddenly exclaimed, "Well look at that, will you?" All three of the occupants in the car were pleased to see Martha beaming with a smile like they hadn't seen in ages, making her way towards them. Gladly realizing that she too, had read some of the journal, for he recognized that glow. Ben quickly got out of the car and opened the rear door for her saying, "Merry Christmas Martha." She put her purse and a bag into the back seat, and then reeling around she gave Ben a big hug saying, "Merry Christmas Ben and thank you so much for Fred's journal! You have no idea how badly I needed that!" Ben felt humbled for a moment, for all he had done was to give her what was rightfully hers anyway, as he looked her in the eyes and returned, "You're quite welcome and actually, I think I did have a fair idea of how much it would help you." Martha hesitated for a bit, studying Ben's face and agreed, "Yes, Benjamin Chambers, I believe that you did!"

Within seconds of pulling out of her driveway, Martha, Sarah, and Helen were lost in endless chatter about some present they had picked out together for Amy. Ben admired the decorations about town as he drove towards their church adding a small comment here and there to the women's conversation. He spent only a few wistful moments wishing that Fred were here to talk to, but he envisioned his gentle friends face wearing a smile which seemed to suggest, "Don't weep for me, I'm just fine." Ben took comfort for the first time since the accident, in realizing that Fred was spending Christmas with Jesus. Ben smiled, but inside he thought, "You may be up in heaven, but I still miss you like crazy, Buddy."

Organ music playing, "O Come All Ye Faithful," filtered out through the church doors as they pulled into the parking lot five minutes later. Salutations of, "Merry Christmas," filled the air as Ben, Sarah, Helen and Martha made their way inside to find Amy and Joe. Ben was pleased to see that they had saved space for them at his favorite pew, the front one, right beneath the church's huge Christmas tree. Ben's parents were sitting beside them on the right. A warm feeling of peace washed over Ben as they, greeted everyone and took their seats. He looked up at the bright shining star atop the tree and his chest swelled with a bit of pride, for he had just stuck it up there a few weeks ago.

Before long the congregation was singing, "Joy to the World," and the children came marching down the center aisle, dressed to play out the parts of the Christmas Nativity story. "Hi, PamPaw," hollered out a certain little smiling, dark curly haired, green eyed, bundle of extreme energy, wearing wings and sporting a halo, as she walked by. Sammi was the prettiest angel Ben had seen since Amy played the part many years ago and Sarah was capturing every second with the cam-corder.

During the program, proud parents, grandparents and parishioners alike chuckled at and cherished the endearing and sometimes comedic performances of the children, while relishing in the joy of the celebration of Christ's birth. Ben held no doubt that it truly was a night that the angelic choirs were singing in Heaven. Near the end of the program, Pastor Rick asked the children to join their families and everyone laughed as Mary, Joseph, shepherds, wise men, costumed animals and all of the different nativity characters scattered throughout the packed sanctuary.

Sammi bounced off the stage and ran over, pouncing into Ben's lap. Her eyes were aglow with excitement as she peered up into his face squealing, "How I do PamPaw?... How I do?" Pure love flowed through Ben's heart as he looked down into his precious angels face and whispered, "You did just great Sammi! I'm so proud of you!" Sammi looked down the pew, past Sarah and Martha to her parents and said, "I do good Mommy!" Amy beamed a smile back at her and softly said, "Yes you did Dear! You did great!" Sarah smiled at her granddaughter and pointing to the cam-corder she added, "And I've got it all right here, you beautiful little angel." Then Pastor Rick said to the congregation, "Now, let us stand and bow our heads for a moment of prayer."

Sammi hopped off of Ben's lap and onto her feet as he got up and with their heads bowed and her tiny hand grasped softly in his own, he focused his attention on the prayer and all of the blessing for which he was thankful this Christmas. The echoes of, "Amen" which soon followed were drowned out by a rich chorus as the organ started to play, "Silent Night," and every light in the room suddenly went out. After a few seconds of darkness, the big star, sitting high atop the huge Christmas tree burst forth in brilliant light. As Ben's eyes adjusted to the light he turned to look at Sarah. Her warm smile made him feel like he was on top of the world. He winked at her, and then clearing his throat, he joined in with the congregation as they started singing, "Silent night. Holy night. All is calm, All is brig..."

Still true to tradition, a few verses were to be sung in German, but even after all of these years, Ben still had not mastered the foreign version of the song. He started out singing okay, "Stille Nacht. Heilige nacht....," but then he was lost and his singing simply turned into humming. As he faked his way through the song, Ben turned and looked at Sarah. He was moved by her beauty and he thanked God that he was the man fortunate enough, to be married to her. Just past Sarah, Martha stood singing and literally glowing with joy. The sparkle in her eyes told Ben, that although Fred was gone, that she was going to be okay. On the other side of Martha, was Helen and she appeared happy as well. Past her, Amy and Joe stood singing, hand in hand and it was easy to see that they were both happy and very much in love. Even Ben's parents at the far end of the pew, appeared to be smiling, as they sang in the darkened chapel.

Ben looked down in front of him at the homemade, sparkling halo sitting atop the curls of his most precious pride and joy. He gently squeezed Sammi's shoulders and she turned looking back up at him with a smile that would have tamed the most savage of beasts, while she sang her own version of the hymn. Ben closed his eyes for a bit and earnestly prayed, "Thank you Lord! Thank you for everything!"

Halfway through the last German verse of, "Silent Night," Ben felt a compelling urge to look at the church's Christmas tree, not just as a casual glance, but to really, look at it. For what seemed like the first time, he noticed and was mesmerized by the contrast of the green needles, the pine cones dangling from it's branches and the glistening beauty of the ornaments as they sparkled in the light of the star overhead.

"How come I've never noticed their brilliance before," Ben wondered with curious speculation. After all, he was one of the church's trustees who helped to hang them up each year. Working his gaze back and forth, up the towering height of the awe-inspiring tree, he became increasingly aware that the star perched on top, appeared to be much brighter than usual. The congregation was now singing in English once more but Ben wasn't even consciously aware of it, so intent was his focus on the star. It was as if he were locked into a deep trance and he made no effort to sing along, nor avert his eyes from its radiant beams. To anyone whom might have been watching, he only appeared to be gazing up at the tree, but something that could only be explained as, "Spiritual," was happening.

Call it a miracle if you wish, but perhaps it was an additional part of the healing Ben needed since losing his best friend, but suddenly, the true meaning of God's immaculate love for mankind, dawned on Ben like it never had before. Somehow he knew that love was larger and more wonderful than anything what could be confined to this world or time as we know it. He realized that if man were left to fend for his own soul's salvation that we all would be doomed, and that only through the birth, death and glorious resurrection of Jesus Christ, God's only Son and our Lord, do we get the opportunity to live forever. Fred had first truly realized that this very evening back in 1972 and now he was experiencing the reality of what his faith had told him ever since.

A joy, far greater than any Ben had ever experienced before instantly warmed his soul and strangely he felt like laughing and crying at the same time, but he did neither. As he stared up at the star, the song ended and the musical voices of the congregation faded away, but the organ continued to softly play. People started to exit the pews and although Ben could sense their movement, he was still frozen in place, looking upward and totally captivated by another vision he was now seeing. He wasn't on medication and it definitely wasn't a mirage, but other than calling it a miracle, how could he ever explain it? Sarah glanced over and thought he was just looking at the star or maybe praying, but Ben was actually seeing something completely amazing, through the glow of the star. He was transfixed on an image that by all logical and reasonable sources of sanity, could not exist, yet it did. He was looking directly through the light of the star at the face of his dear departed friend, Fred, only he wasn't dead. He was alive, with a magnificent aura shining about him and smile stretched from ear to ear.

Ben was nearly overcome with joy as Fred nodded at him. He seemed both far away and near at the same time. His lips were not moving, but oddly, as if through some unexplainable form of mental telepathy, Ben could hear his familiar, deep countrified voice saying, "Ya got ta' git back ta' livin' Ben, an' let me go. Hev' sum' fun, an' laugh agin'." Then his voice lost it's twang and he said, "I'm home now and it's amazing, Ben! Don't you see, that day I left, it wasn't, Good Bye! It was just the beginning of Forever. I'll meet up with you later!"

The vision faded nearly as fast as it had appeared, but the joy which had been implanted inside of Ben's heart did not. He jumped, startled a bit when Sarah grasped his arm and asked, "Ben? Honey, are you okay?" Turning to her, with the reality of what he had just witnessed sinking in, and realizing that Fred was happily where we all eventually long to be, Ben looked Sarah in the eyes, and spoke the truest words he had ever uttered when he replied, "Everything is just great!" In his heart, it truly was and he felt like shouting with joy.

Ben could have left the church that night thinking he was the only one who saw Fred smiling beyond the star's light, but then he happened to notice Sammi. She was gazing upward, towards the star and her lips were moving. He knelt down on one knee beside her and although he already had a fair idea of what her answer would be, he asked, "Sammi, Honey? Who are you talking to?" Her gaze continued upward and her lips kept moving for about five seconds before she turned with a huge smile saying, "I was telwin' Fwed, Mewy' Cwismas', PamPaw!" A shudder of odd emotion trembled through Ben's body as he realized his intuition was right and he pulled his cute little darling close, for a hug. Looking upward he smiled, and although he could no longer see Fred, he felt his presence nearby and the immeasurable love of Christ, surged deep inside his being. Then rising to his feet, Ben winked towards Heaven and uttered, "Merry Christmas Fred!"

Picking up Sammi in one arm and while hugging Sarah with the other he said, "Well, Sweetheart, are you and Sammi ready to go home and see if we can find some presents?" Sarah just smiled as Sammi squirmed and shouted, "Pwesents! Yay," and together they and the rest of their clan, exited the pew. As they made their way down the church aisle exchanging holiday greetings with everyone, Ben realized something. Forever forth, from this glorious night, he would be able to tell people, "Yes, Jesus is real and miracles do occur! Life may not always appear to be fair, but it does go on." Ben felt a little foolish, for he had been spending his time trying to be sad for so long that he had forgotten about just how good, God's love can be. Bad things do happen in life, that's just the way it is and we will not always figure out the answers to the proverbial question of, "Why?" but that is never an excuse for us to give up on life.

There is far more to God's plan than the existence we have in the here and now. Ben now realizes that his focus shouldn't be on the sadness of losing Fred, but on the blessings he received through being his friend. The good times, love and laughter personally spent with him can be replayed in memory or in conversation with others anytime and even death cannot take that away. Sure it will still hurt and be troubling at times, but that's okay because like Fred once said, "It all be part of da' journey."

Back in 1972, on Christmas Eve, a stranger named Frederic F. Stone, first came to a little church and sat next to a man named, Ben Chambers. By the end of the service a miracle had occurred. A tormented soul had been redeemed and several wonderful relationships had begun. At the beginning of that amazing evening Fred had owned nothing more than rags, dirt, a small knapsack, a journal, and a ton of haunted memories, but after some divine intervention, he received salvation and became a new man. Salvation for the world first came on a special, lonely night in Bethlehem many years ago in the form, not of a conquering king, but as a newborn babe. He came bearing no weapons and leading no army, yet because of that baby, the battle against sin was inevitably, already won. He brought with him the free gift of eternal life.

To receive this most perfect of gifts was meant to be as simple as believing and opening one's heart, but for many people, that is difficult to do. Fred, prior to that Christmas Eve, was one of those people, naturally good on the inside, but so torn up by the circumstances of life that he had given up hope. It was in his greatest personal moment of spiritual weakness, when he had no will left inside, that the true love and grace of God came shining through and redeemed him. God knows the very things which weigh down our souls and he longs to lift us up, just as he did Fred back then and Ben tonight.

A lost soul's salvation became a reality on that wonderful night thirty-four years ago. When he had found himself at the end of his rope, as a dirty and ragged, emotionally torn vagabond amongst a room full of believers. He opened his heart and bared his soul, relinquishing years of pain and sorrow, right there under the lighted star of Jesus. He was the complete stranger who miraculously found himself, became a true friend, and was a stranger no more. On that night, he wandered into a strange community which became his new home. There he prepared himself to one day leave this life, to enter into Heaven's forevermore. Ben's heart expanded with joy as he walked down the church aisle and contemplated all of this. He realized that it was okay to be saddened by losing Fred, but there was something that far outweighed the tragedy. It was how richly he had been blessed to be able to walk part of Fred's spiritual journey with him.

As he was exiting the church, holding both Sarah and Sammi's hands and wishing everyone a, "Merry Christmas," Ben felt great. He looked back, behind Sarah at Martha. She still wore a smile that told him she fully realized the truth as well and although there were still going to be tough days, and more tears to be shed, that she was going to make it just fine. Amy and Joe, along with Ben's folks, went out ahead of them and promised to meet them at the house. Both Sammi and Ben's eyes lit up as they received their bags of goodies at the back of the church, just before shaking hands with Pastor Rick. Stepping out into the cool refreshing night air, Ben noticed that the snow had stopped falling and a thin new blanket of white covered the ground under the bright light of a full December moon and millions of twinkling stars.

Martha is no longer hurting and Ben is at peace with himself, and with God. The light of spiritual happiness can be seen shining in all of their faces. The one person who appears to be missing from their family circle isn't really gone at all. He will always be in their memories and hearts until that glorious day when they see him again. Rest assured that the small man with the giant voice, and even larger heart, is smiling from ear to ear, in the very place that all true Christian long to one day be. Frederick Flint Stone is smack dab in heaven's domain, basking in the glow of the presence of Jesus Christ the Lord.

Ben took a deep breath, liking the feel of the cold night air in his lungs. Car after car was pulling out of the church parking lot, making fresh tracks in the snow as an almost magical sense of excitement filled the air. As they descended the church's steps, and started towards their car, Ben looked up, just in time to see a shooting star go whizzing by. "See you later Buddy," he whispers thinking of Fred. Then, for just a moment, he imagines he can hear Fred's deep voice holler, "Merry Christmas Ya'll," followed by the joyous singing of cardinals. "It most certainly has been a time of miracles," thinks Ben. Sammi's high-pitched voice suddenly cuts into the night and echoes across the snow. "Wook PamPaw! Can-y Canes, wook!" Ben looks down at Sammi, who is still standing beside him and smiles as she unwraps the red and white striped, peppermint treat from her goodie bag and pops it into her mouth.

"Hey, look over there, Sammi," Ben exclaims, pointing at a rabbit as it takes off from between two parked cars next to them. "Bunny PamPaw! Wook MamMaw, Bunny! Martha, MamMaw Helwin, wook! See the bunny," Sammi squeals with excitement while they all stand watching it bound off across the parking lot, kicking up spurts of white fluff. As the rabbit disappears, Ben digs into his own bag of goodies and finds a candy cane. Unwrapping it, he holds it up in front of himself while smiling down at Sammi. She smiles back, and Ben motions with the candy and asks, "What does the, "J" mean Sammi?" Everyone laughs as Sammi pulls her own candy cane out of her mouth saying, "Mmmmm! Fwed says "J" is fo' Jesus an' he's Goooooood!" Ben slowly looks upward once more and winks toward the sky as he adds, "Yes Sammi, he surely is!"

"Amen," the others add. Ben exhales and can see his breath in the cool night air, but he is warm on the inside. At least for that moment, all of the pain and sorrow is gone and everything feels better than great,... it is perfectly right.

EPILOGUE

"Pop, pop, pop, pop, pop, pop, pop,... Pow!... Boooooom!"
The hungry coyote winces at the sounds of the fireworks going off, as he warily and cautiously makes his way through the weeds along the swollen river's bank. Suddenly, he freezes in place, growling slightly as his ears perk up, he bares his teeth, and the fur stands up on his back. Just ahead of him, in the clearing he can see the one thing which scares him far more than the loud noises, bright colorful lights, and the smell of sulfur floating in the air,... It's the humans.

He knew they were here long before he saw them, for he could smell and hear them, yet seeing them now with his own eyes, instantly sends waves of sheer terror coursing through his long, lean body. His kind and theirs have never gotten along and he learned long ago, as a young pup, to keep his distance from these dangerous two-legged creatures. He has seen many of his brethren fall at their destructive hands.

There are literally hundreds of them here tonight, standing, sitting, talking, yelling, feasting, and celebrating as they watch the strange, loud lights in the sky. The large objects they arrive in are parked in long rows, side by side, at one edge of the clearing. He has been to this spot many times before, but only in the late hours of the night, when he can roll in the short, soft grass without fearing for his safety, when no one is around.

This clearing is a strange place, full of things he does not understand like playground equipment, picnic tables and shelters, horseshoe pits, grills, roads, and his favorite object here, garbage cans. Hidden within these strange metal containers he has always been able to find, what desperation has driven him here for tonight,... nourishment. The wonderful smells of grilled brats, dogs, chicken, steaks and burgers has been drifting upstream for hours and to a hungry mongrel like the famished coyote, it had been pure torture. He had no control and could not resist when his nose led him to this spot tonight, yet he still possesses the innate wisdom to exercise patience. He can wait for the people to leave and wishes none of then any harm. In fact, he gives them little personal thought at all. He is simply here wanting that which they have, and he desperately needs, wonderful, glorious,... food.

He crouches down low behind a stand of cattails not more than twenty-five feet from the nearest group of the people. There are five of the larger ones sitting in lawn chairs and a small female one with a high-pitched voice standing beside the one on the left. Several crickets move away from him and a frog jumps into the water of the river, but he pays no attention to them. He lies unmoving, still as a stone, yet he is fully alert, smelling, listening and watching. No one is aware of the brave predator in their midst, and usually he would never allow them to get so close, but it has been days since he has eaten anything more than an insect or two. Hunger drives him to do what he must.

"Wook' PamPaw, Look," shouts Sammi with a hotdog in one hand and pointing with the other to the red, white, and blue starburst in the sky. "Fireworks pretty," she states with a smile. "Yes they are, and so are you Dear," Ben thinks to himself as he looks at his grandaughter and smiles. He is amazed at how much her talking has improved in just the last seven months and she seems to be growing like a weed. In the glow cast by the next brilliant blast high overhead, Ben looks to his side at Sarah and thinks she looks absolutely beautiful. Seated next to her is Martha of course and Amy and Joe are sitting on the end closest to the weeds.

Every year they come to this very spot in the "State Park," to watch the fireworks on the Fourth of July, but for a while no one thought they would be able to this year. Over the last few months it has rained excessively and the river was in danger of flooding. Fortunately however, it hasn't rained for over a week now, and although the swift, dangerous, debris-filled waters of the river are only a foot or two from where they are sitting right now, they are gradually receding and no longer rising. All activities on the water were banned for the holiday because of the swift currents and the dangerous undertow, but picnicking and games carried on all day in the park just as in every other year.

Patriotic music is blaring from speakers situated all about the park and several vendors are selling food and drink. The hot dog Sammi is carrying is her third for the evening and right now Ben is teasing her. "Hey Sammi, why don't you give your old grandpa here, your hot dog. It sure looks good." Sammi turns away from him quickly, laughs and squeals, "No PamPaw! Save my hot dog, Daddy," as she runs down to Joe who's sitting closest to the cattails and weeds. Although he can't hear them over all the noise, Ben quickly surmises that Sammi's father is teasing her about her hot dog as well. Sammi smiles big, turns away from Joe, saying something while shaking her head and she starts back towards Ben.

Suddenly, thunderous explosions shake the ground and brilliant burst of color light up the sky like the noonday sun, signifying the fireworks grand finale. Muted "ooh's," and "aah's," resonate all around Ben as everyone watches the spectacular display. Ben begins to turn his head as well, but before he can look upward, he sees something that nearly causes his heart to stop beating. Everything goes completely silent and starts moving in slow motion. Ben himself is frozen, unable to yell or move, watching in horror, as Sammi turns in mid stride to look up. Her foot slips on something in the grass and her face becomes a mask of terror as her hot dog goes flying through the air and she plunges backwards into the swift, cold, dark water of the river and disappears from sight.

Fear, far greater than he has ever known envelops Ben and he tries to jump up out of his chair, but he cannot move. Only seconds pass, but it seems like an eternity before he can finally make it to his feet screaming, "Saaaaaaammi!" No one else noticed for they all were watching the glorious display high over their heads, but at Ben's horrific cry they all lunge to their feet in a panic instantly realizing that Sammi is no longer there. Sarah, Martha and Amy scream in terror as they realize what has happened and Ben, just a step ahead of Joe, frantically starts to step forward to dive into the river after Sammi. Before he can jump however a figure rushes past him, springs into the air and disappears below the surface of the river's treacherous waters. More people catch on to what has just happened as Ben and his family start running down along the river's edge, screaming for Sammi and desperately trying to see something in the darkness. "God no! Not Sammi! God please save her! Please God, where is she," Ben yells as he anxiously rushes along the shore, pushing his way through crowds of people who don't know what has happened and are still watching the fireworks. Almost a hundred yards down from where they had been sitting Ben stops, bends over breathing hard and peers out into the water still seeing nothing. He screams Sammi's name over and over again, and soon Sarah, Amy, Joe and Martha along with dozens of other people are all doing the same. "Where is she?" Amy shrieks straining to see something, anything at all. She turns to Joe who is as scared and feeling as helpless as Ben and throws herself into his arms screaming in agony.

Ben is prepared to jump into the river, but where? "God, where is she? Where's my Sammi" he shouts to the sky still straining to see as Sarah buries her head in his chest and cries. Martha is standing at the edge of the water calling Sammi's name and suddenly, in his mind, Ben saw the same big fish he saw in his dream, the night before Fred died and what happened next, scared him even more than he already was. Just as in the dream, the fish jumped out of the water and looked at him with it's one big eye. Again the eye seemed to glow with intelligence and it blinked, but that vision was not the source of the cold fear that washed over Ben, it was the voice that followed. He heard Sammi's voice utter the same words she did in the dream, "Don't worry PamPaw, Jesus told me, evwythin' will be all-wight!" Ben nearly screamed, instantly assuming that what he heard meant that Sammi was going to heaven, just like Fred. There was no way he was ready to let go, and he silently pleaded desperately and vehemently with God. "Please God, not again... not Sammi! No, it's not fair! God, it's just not fair! You've got to save her... You have too!"

Ben eyes filled with tears as he looked up still internally yelling at God, "No, you can't have her! You can't do this to us! Not again God, not little Sammi! Please God, no!... Not Sammi!" Half dragging Sarah he wandered down the bank still searching the black surface of the water and for some unknown reason, he remembered part of the letter that Fred had left him in the journal. Confusion clouded Ben's mind as these words seemed to holler out to him, "It ain't at all, bout' bein' fair. It's bout' livin', not jest' now, but fo'eva." Ben looked up to heaven again feeling like he was going insane wondering what God was trying to tell him. Then suddenly, a woman standing just ten feet from Ben and Sarah yelled, "There they are!"

Everyone looked in the direction the woman was excitedly pointing. At first Ben saw nothing, but then just fifty feet out in the water, he thought he could make out something moving and slowly growing closer. "Oh my God, he's got her. It's Sammi, Joe! Thank God it's Sammi," Amy's voice shot out all at once and everyone anxiously moved to the very edge of the water.

About ten seconds later a teenage boy staggered ashore pulling Sammi with him and aside from being winded and soaked to the bone, they were both fine. Shouts of joy and cheers went up all around as Sammi cried safe and secure in her mother's arms while Joe stood by their side with tears of immaculate joy running from his eyes and he kept saying, "thank you," to the young man who had risked his own life in the dangerous waters of the river to save their precious daughter. Martha was next to them, looking to the sky thanking God, while Ben and Sarah held on to each other crying as well and rendered up their own thanks and praise. After a few minutes Sammi stopped crying and Ben and Sarah were able to hug her too. Within minutes she was laughing and smiling just like she had been before the accident and a great sense of relief washed over Ben as he watched her. "I love her so much Lord, thank you!" All at once Sammi came up to Ben and tugged on his hand saying, "PamPaw." Ben knelt down and hugged her, planting a big kiss on her forehead and then he replied, "What is it Princess?" Sammi smiled at him and then looking to his side, her adorable face literally started glowing as she pointed behind Ben and said, "PamPaw, he saved me."

Instantly Ben knew that he owed someone else a great debt of gratitude. He stood up, grasping Sammi's hand and turned around. The fireworks had ended by now, but the parks lights provided enough light for Ben to see a soaking wet young man approaching from out of the shadows. Sarah came up and swept Sammi up in her arms smothering her with hugs and kisses as Ben reached his hand out to the hero who had saved his grandaughter. Now that he was up close enough to see clearly, the rescuer looked strangely familiar to Ben, but he couldn't place him. He must have only been fifteen or sixteen, and Ben figured the smiling couple standing a few feet behind the boy were his proud parents. "I should know this kid," he thought to himself. As they shook hands and Ben introduced himself and thanked him over and over again for saving Sammi, he couldn't shake the feeling that he somehow knew the boy. Finally, curiosity got the best of him and he said, "Thank you again young man, but I feel like I've met you before. What's your name?" The boy's parents walked up as the boy replied, "Mr. Chambers, we've never met before, but... you have seen me." Curiosity filled Ben's mind as the boy's father and mother walked up and said, "Well Logan are you going to introduce us?" At the mention of the name "Logan," Ben stared at the boy even more convinced that he knew him, but how? Logan smiled and said, "Mr. Chambers, I'd like you to meet my parents, Bruce and Lori Wilson."

"Logan, Logan Wilson," the name repeated in Ben's mind as he shook hands with the lads parents. He turned to look at the boy and he had his hand to his face, brushing aside his wet hair back from his forehead and all at once two things happened in Ben's mind. First, he had another vision of the past. The vision was from a very special day back on the 9th of September 2002. Ben and his best friend Fred were standing outside a nursery room window at the hospital staring a a beautiful newborn baby girl named "Samantha Marie Welsh." Ben felt warm all over as once again he heard Fred's deep gentle voice speaking to the baby. "Ah's gonna call ya' Sammi, L'il Darlin', an' ah'll make ya' dis' promise. Ole' Fred'll make sho' ya' stays safe an' thet' nuttin' bad e'er happens ta' ya'!" The vivid recollection of Fred's promise came to Ben in an instant, no longer than the single flap of a hummingbird's wings. Then secondly, the even more amazing thing he suddenly realized, was that he did know who the boy was. A bolt of awe inspiring revelation flowed through Ben's mind even before the boy said, "Mr. Chambers, I'm the one your friend saved last September."

Later when Ben shares the news with the rest of the family and Martha they will be nearly as amazed as he was, especially when Ben goes on to tell them about Fred's promise, of how he did indeed, through saving Logan, whom in turn saved Sammi, keep his promise and kept something bad from happening to her. Despite all the sadness and pain they have been through since Fred died they will be able to see his love live on through Sammi every day until the time comes for them to join Fred in the light of Jesus love up above.

The 4th of July will forever be a glorious day of celebration for Joe, Amy and Sammi, for Ben and Sarah and for Martha. It won't just be for "Independence Day" and the freedoms enjoyed in our great country which has been granted to us through the blood and sacrifices of American soldiers, but it will be a celebration of Sammi's rescue and the life they and all believers will enjoy, not just in the "Here and now," but in the knowledge that we can inherit life eternal through the blood, sacrifice and resurrection of Christ Jesus, God's only Son and our Lord.

It is nearly midnight now and all the people have gone. The flashes of fireflies shine here and there as the calls of frogs, crickets, crayfish, and whippoorwills blend together to serenade the night. Occasionally the call of a screech owl adds to the late night choir. A faint smell of sulfur still clings to the air and the sound of the rivers rushing water is soothing to the ears of the coyote. For now he is content and all around him, each of the creatures of the night do what they must to survive. He has already rolled in the lush grass of the clearing and searched all around the things of man which he doesn't understand. He is no longer hungry for he has satisfied his hunger with what was left behind. Perhaps the tastiest morsel he partook of this evening wasn't the half eaten chicken breast he found or even the burgers or brats lying all about. The one thing he enjoyed the most, was the first bit of food he was able to obtain.

It was hours ago, when he was settled down low to the ground behind the cattails watching the closest group of the humans, the five with the little female. She was excited with a high pitched voice, running from one end of her group and back again and again. It wasn't her excitement which had drawn the wild canine's attention however, it was what she had held in her hands. Better yet, at least from his hungry perspective, it was what flew out of her hands when she went into the water. The coyote wished the little human no harm, and it would be wonderful to say that he was happy when she was later rescued, but he really never knew. When all of the people were rejoicing over her rescue, he too was rejoicing a safe distance away in his own unique way. He was eating Sammi's hotdog.

Miles away now, Ben Chambers is sleeping peacefully next to his beautiful bride of over forty-four years. There was a time, not too long ago when he could not sleep and he was hurting over the loss of someone he and his family loved dearly. For a long time he fought his emotions and he even was angry with God.

He still misses his friend, but now he knows, that's okay. He has witnessed miracles and realizes that he has been given more cause to rejoice than he has had, to grieve. When he was still stuck in his anger and confusion he refused to view the bigger picture, but now he knows what lies ahead. It took some time, and the way was hard to travel for him to get to this point, but Ben, just like any of us can do with the Lord's guidance, figured out the way. He stopped just making a statement and found his own answers for the question that should have followed the statement all along. It only took searching his heart to realize he already knew the answer that could make him feel better, he just wasn't accept it, but now he has. Ben would challenge any of us going through difficult times to really ponder that which he eventually figured out, "God it's just not fair!... Or, is is?"

Printed in the United States
205396BV00001B/373-414/P